MW00885332

Surviving 7 Years with Rice and Beans

The Prepper's Cookbook on Stockpile Food to Be Totally Prepared for Any Emergency

TABLE OF CONTENTS

Book 1
Disaster Preparation

Introduction

Preppers have always existed to some degree, and today more than ever, people are turning to books like this one in order to acquire the necessary knowledge to survive an apocalyptic situation. Humanity has seen many close calls over the course of its history, from wars to economic collapse, and even pandemics. Although many prepper books are centered on surviving in the wild, we realize that if a catastrophe were to happen, most of us will find ourselves in an urban environment. This is not to say that many of the same techniques will not apply, but you need to be able to adapt to the environment you live in, take advantage of it, and understand which strategies may or may not work in it.

In this book, we will go through many different situations, and how you can respond to them. It is important to build a base and fortify it and to build a sustainable source of food. But most importantly you must build your stockpile of goods, medication, and tools that you will need in order to survive for as long as you can. In these scenarios, we always expect help to come eventually, in whatever form, or for civilization to restore itself. We don't think about the possibility that help may not come, partly because it is an extremely frightening prospect and partly because it isn't that likely. Humans are extremely adaptable and have always found their way back. In a disaster situation we can expect civilization to be restored, eventually.

In any case, in this book, you will find the information you need to survive prolonged periods of time without contact with civilization, and to build a sustainable source of food that can last for many years. You will learn about building shelters, putting together first aid kits, how to stockpile and how to build a survival garden. We hope, of course, to never have to use these skills, but the world is unpredictable, and it is always best to be prepared.

Chapter 1: Disaster Preparation

Making a Plan

Making a plan is the first step to being ready for any disaster, regardless of what disaster that may be. There are several things that you and your family or friends all need to be aware of in case you are not all together when an emergency strikes.

The first thing you should all be aware of is the different warnings and emergency alerts that you may receive. Usually, when an emergency happens, safety officials have a number of different ways to alert you. When you receive an alert, you will usually have enough time to gather everything you need. Below is a breakdown of the various alerts you may receive:

Wireless Emergency Alerts (WEAs)

Wireless Emergency Alerts are usually short messages that are sent from an official authority be that federal, state, local, or regional. They are transmitted from cell towers.
Usually, these alerts are sent out to people if they are in danger or potentially in danger. This could be both man-made or natural disasters.

Depending on the emergency, there are several types of wireless emergency alerts; AMBER (America's Missing: Broadcast Emergency Response) Alerts, Imminent Threat Alerts, Public Safety Alerts, or Presidential alerts.

Amber Alert

The Amber Alert is the most frequent type of alert. It is sent out to the public when a local child has been abducted. The speed of these alerts is oftentimes crucial to returning the child home safely. The aim of an Amber Alert is to instruct the local community to assist in locating the child.

Public Safety Alert

A public safety alert is sent out when a threat has passed or is not imminent. This could include natural disasters or other human-related situations.

Imminent Threat Alerts

These are more severe than public safety alerts and are sent out when you are directly in harm's way. Again, the threat could be man-made or natural such as extreme weather.

Presidential Alerts

These alerts are only sent when a national disaster or emergency occurs. They are sent out nationwide so anyone with a cell phone is able to receive it.

There are several things that you need to know about WEA alerts. Firstly, they are messages that appear on your phone screen and let you know the type of threat at hand, as well as any action that you should follow. It is a small message, no longer than 360 characters.

These alerts have a unique vibration and tone so they are easily recognizable. They are broadcasted through local cell towers so anyone near it will receive it and the congestion of phone networks does not affect the time it takes for the message to be delivered.

Because of the way these alerts are sent, you can receive them if there's a threat where you are, even if you don't live nearby. These alerts are based on your current location.

Emergency Alert System (EAS)
EAS are national public warnings and are designed to allow the president to address the nation within 10 minutes when the country is under a national emergency.

However, the president is not the only one who can access this system; these alerts can be issued by local and state authorities in order to give out weather warnings, AMBER alerts, and imminent threat warnings.

This system is operated by the FCC, the Federal Emergency Management Agency (FEMA), and the National Oceanic and Atmospheric Administration's National Weather Service (NWS). They maintain the EAS, as well as coordinate WEA warnings, making them the two main bodies responsible for maintaining national security.

NOAA Weather Radio (NWR)
The NOAA Weather Radio is a nationwide radio broadcast, as well as a radio network where information about extreme weather is announced, but it also broadcasts other emergencies such as national security threats or public safety.

Working with FCC, the NWR's broadcast makes it a one-stop-shop for finding out any weather-related issues that might be taking place in the country.

Shelter Plan

Sheltering is almost always appropriate in emergency or disaster situations. Seeking shelter is usually done at the home, office, or any other location if danger is imminent and there is not time for you to go to a safer place.

The time you spend sheltering may vary depending on the emergency. You need to stay informed in order to estimate how long you might have to shelter for and how strictly to ration your supplies. Making sure you, your family, or friends have the necessities to survive, such as food and water, is essential, especially if the sheltering time is undefined.

When sheltering, there are two main courses of action depending on the emergency and where you are: going to a Mass Care Shelter or sheltering in place. Here are the main differences and how you should proceed in each situation.

Mass Care Shelters

Although most Mass Care Shelters provide supplies such as food and water, you should take your emergency kit with you. Usually, these places are crowded with little to no room, and having all your necessities with you is a great advantage.

In a Mass Care Shelter, you should also bring hygiene products, such as sanitizers, soaps, and other general cleaning products.

If you are in the US, you can find your nearest shelter by texting SHELTER followed by your zip code to 43362.

Sheltering in Place

Often, when an emergency strikes, you should stay where you are, especially if going outside seems risky. You always need to be prepared to take shelter where you are at the moment of disaster. This could be at home, in your office, or in any other building. If you haven't received an alert but think that there might be a dangerous situation arising, you need to use your common sense and assess the situation carefully. This might happen if local or national authorities cannot immediately provide you with information about what is happening. Here are some tips on how to behave in such a situation:

- Try to stay informed, by watching TV, listening to the radio, or following information on your cell phone.

- Close windows, lock doors, and air vents, as well as any other openings such as fireplaces.

- Turn off any other system that might circulate air between the outside and inside such as air conditioning or fans.

- Find a place with as few windows as possible.

- Seal windows, doors, and vents with plastic sheeting.

Evacuation Plan

Before and During Evacuation

Planning for an emergency also means planning for an evacuation. In some situations, you may have time to take your time, in others you may have to evacuate immediately.

You need to understand what kind of emergency you are in in order to correctly prepare for an evacuation. After that, you need to identify what places are available for you to evacuate to, such as community shelters, a family or friend's home in another city, or even a hotel. Knowing alternate routes in your area and how to procure various means of transportation can also help you evacuate in a safer, faster way. Keep in mind, that depending on the situation, evacuating on foot might be the best option. You should also have a plan in place to meet up with your family or have a way to contact them in case you become separated.

It is important to have an emergency kit, or a "go-bag" ready in case you need to leave on foot. It should contain supplies that will last you a long time, such as canned goods. It may be possible to evacuate by car, so you should keep an emergency kit in your car at all times and make sure that tank of gas is consistently topped up as gas stations may be closed during an emergency.

During an evacuation, it's important to remember to take with you a battery-powered radio. You should have already downloaded the FEMA app so you know where open shelters are in your area. If you have pets, keep in mind that most public shelters only allow service dogs.

If you have the time, you should try to secure your home by locking doors and windows, unplugging any electrical appliances such as TVs and microwaves, and if you are instructed to, shut off your gas, electricity, and water. However, this might not be needed in all cases. Leave home with thick shoes, or boots, long pants, and long-sleeved shirts so you have extra protection outside.

Before leaving, you should check if your neighbors might need a ride. If your car is full, try to provide them with some supplies if they need them, or arrange for someone to pick them up.

After Evacuation

Before returning from an evacuation, make sure your national or regional authorities have given the green light. Ensure that there is no debris or any other disruptions on the road on your way back.

Bring supplies, such as water and food for your return and if you are coming back by car, make sure you don't run out of fuel, or ensure there will be a gas station open. Avoid downed power lines as these might still be live, if you encounter any, call the emergency services to inform them.

If you return home and you have no power, you can use generators, but it is important to know that you shouldn't use these inside your home or connect them to the electrical system in your house. If you need to use a generator, connect it to an external electrical plug.

If You Are Evacuating with Pets

Making a plan for your pet will enable you to execute a smoother evacuation. It is important to note that many public shelters do not allow pets, which can cause you a lot of stress in an emergency situation. Knowing what you are going to do with your pet before emergency strikes can save their life. Establish an evacuation plan with your neighbors or friends in case you are unable to evacuate your pet yourself. Also, having your pet microchipped can be very helpful if it ever gets lost.

You should also put together an emergency kit for your pet, as you would for you and your family. This shouldn't differ much from your own emergency kit; you will need food, water, medicine if your pet needs it, and a first aid kit. You should also include an ID tag and a leash, as well as your pet's information and any other important medical documents.

Ideally, you would place your pet in a crate or a carrier and make sure you put in items or toys that your pet is familiar with, as this often helps them reduce their stress.

If your animals or pets can't be put in a carrier because of their size, evacuate them as soon as you can in vehicles or trailers. Make sure the place where you are taking them can meet your animal's basic needs, such as water, food, and veterinary care.

If you have large farm animals such as cows or horses and you cannot evacuate them, you should put them inside a barn or another large building, or if you think the emergency at hand will destroy the barn/building, you should set them loose as they may have a better chance of surviving.

Building a Kit

When a disaster or emergency strikes, we won't know what to expect. Worst case scenario, we could be on our own for several days before returning to safety. This means that a well-built disaster kit is essential. You will need some basic items and some additional emergency supplies. Here's a comprehensive list of supplies:

Basic Items

- Water (aim to have a gallon per person/day)
- Food (several days'-supply)
- Battery-powered radio and a NOAA radio
- First aid kit
- Extra batteries
- Flashlight
- Duct tape and plastic sheeting
- Dust mask
- Pliers or a wrench
- Can opener
- Local maps
- Cell phone with backup batteries

These are items that you should always have with you in an emergency, however, if you can, you should add these extra items to your kit:

Additional Supplies

- Prescribed medication
- Eyeglasses or contact lenses if you need
- Cash
- Sleeping bag or blankets
- Matches
- Personal identification documents
- Fire extinguisher

You should make your emergency kit and keep it in a safe place for when you might need it. Make sure to store your kit in an appropriate place, for example, canned food needs to be kept in a dry place. You should also replace any expired items and go through all the emergency items to make sure they are still intact and change them if necessary.

Because you don't know when an emergency will strike, you should prepare at least three different emergency kits; one for your home, one for your car, and one for your workplace.

Survival Kit for the Injured

Many of us might have an issue with turning away people that seek our help, especially if they are badly wounded. If this is the case with you, then you can put together a charity survival kit. Obviously, only do this if you have enough supplies for yourself and your family. Here's a list of what you might want to include:

- a couple of bottles of water
- a couple of cans of food with a can opener
- an emergency blanket
- a map with directions to the nearest shelter
- a set of clean clothes
- a few strike-everywhere matches

Place these items in a plastic bag so they don't get wet and place them anywhere outside your perimeter (we will talk about this later in the book). If someone comes close to your perimeter and you feel the need to help them, tell them where the charity kit is.

Making a plan ahead of time is one of the most important things you can do. If an emergency situation strikes, and you don't have a plan, chances are that you will not survive long. These types of plans require a lot of thinking, time to stockpile goods and medical items and they cannot be rushed. Without a plan, you will be lost.

It is important to understand the first signs of an emergency, such as understanding the different alerts and how to proceed when one is issued. There are a few different ones and depending on which one is sent, you should know what to do next. Along with a general plan for emergency situations, you should also have a shelter plan, for both short and long term, whether it is a government shelter or your own home. An evacuation plan is also essential when a local catastrophe strikes; knowing where to go, whether it is a family member's house or a friend's house that is far from yours and far from the emergency. You need to prepare for these situations and have an evacuation kit that is already assembled, so all you need to do is grab it and leave your home.

Being prepared is really important when it comes to surviving emergency situations, and the truth is, you can never be too prepared.

Chapter 2: Prepper's Long-Term Survival Guide

If a major disaster happens, we may need to be in survival mode for the long-term, or at least be prepared for that scenario. For these scenarios to play out, the catastrophes need to be big enough to bring society to a halt. This would certainly bring about lot of chaos and confusion.

Fortunately, these situations almost never happen, but it is always better to be prepared in case one does happen someday. Before we go through what we should do in a worst-case scenario, let us talk about the different situations we may find ourselves in. You will have to behave slightly differently depending on the type of catastrophe.

Famine

Famine is a severe lack of food that spreads nationwide or worldwide. There are many reasons this could happen, massive crop failure, or a situation where the amount of available food decreases sharply. Examples of this could be a disease affecting crops, a long drought or flooding, for example, back in 1995, a series of floods brought food shortages to North Korea. Sometimes political measures can also affect food distribution.

Another infamous case was the Irish Potato Famine which occurred between 1845 and 1852 and killed around one million people. This was caused by a disease in the potatoes, but the biggest issue here was the lack of food diversity - most of the population came to rely on one variety of potatoes, the Irish Lumper. Other diseases started to spread as a result of people's failing immune systems and the lack of medical care and other basic necessities.

Fortunately, we have learned from those mistakes and we grow different varieties of crops to try and prevent famine from occurring. However, in this era of global warming and climate change, a similar situation could happen.

Pandemic

This one might still be fresh in the mind for many of us, but the pandemic that occurred in 2019, due to a spread of a flu-like disease, doesn't really compare to other pandemics throughout our history. A pandemic is when a large number of people throughout a large area, or across a number of countries are affected by the same disease.

One of the worst pandemics affecting humanity was the Black Plague, where reports say that around 200 million people died between 1347 and 1350. That was about 60 percent of the world population at the time. Historians believe this plague started near China and was transported to Europe in ships and other routes, through fleas on rats.

There have been other cases throughout history, more recently during World War I, when there was an outbreak of the H1N1 flu virus otherwise known as the Spanish flu. This flu pandemic was particularly scary because it affected healthy young adults more severely because the healthier the person was, the harder the flu attacked.

Economic Collapse

An economic collapse is quite a hard concept to define when compared to other disasters, mainly because many things could fall under the term. For example, economic depression, hyperinflation, mass unemployment or mass bankruptcies.

A recent example of this was when Russia's economy collapsed in 1998. At the time, banks closed and people panic-bought goods. Inflation increased more than 80%. While the country was going through that, the value of the ruble, Russia's currency, crashed. People living in urban areas had no means to get food and had to wait in hour-long lines to get something to eat.

Terrorism and War

Depending on where you live, terrorism and war could still be a real threat. The events of 9/11 for instance, changed how the U.S dealt with terrorism and its own security. And the possibility of war can never be taken off the table.

Although this might be hard to imagine for some, one has to be prepared for any events that might disturb our way of life.

None of this means that events like this will happen any time soon, or even in your lifetime but it is savvy to make preparations and take the necessary steps to increase your chances of survival in case war does break out.

Water Procurement

The human body can survive without water for about three days; however, chances are, in a disaster situation people won't survive that long without water. Regular consumption of water is essential to maintain your healthy body and keep your mind sharp.

We need water for hygiene purposes too, which means that humans use quite a lot of water in a single day, about a hundred gallons to be precise. The problem in a disaster situation is often not the scarcity of water in general, but the scarcity of potable water. So, in case of an emergency, you need to have quite a lot more water than you think if you want to survive long term.

In a disaster situation, there are four possible types of water source; your own water reserves, rainwater, drilled wells, and natural resources, such as lakes or rivers.

Storing Water

If you want to store water for an emergency, you need to plan beforehand. Water can be quite the load to carry, both because it's heavy and because it takes up space. Everyone can move a gallon of water; however, the issue is when you need to carry other items too. There are some great products out there that can help you carry large amounts of water and which would certainly be a good addition to your survival kit. Nevertheless, this doesn't change the fact that it is still heavy and takes up a lot of space.

Having access to even a small reserve of water is extremely important, but moving large quantities of it, especially in an emergency, is not very feasible. But if you keep a static storage of water, you will find it easier to collect some if you need to evacuate in a hurry. However, if you have a static source of water, you need to store it properly so it doesn't go rancid and make sure you rotate your water at least every six months.

Disinfecting and storing water

If you don't have access to bottled water, you can use tap water, however, you might need to disinfect your water before you store it so that bacteria and viruses don't multiply once it is stored. The simplest way to do this is by boiling the water. This is enough to kill any bacteria, pathogens, or viruses. If you're taking water from natural sources, let it sit for a minute before you filter it using a towel, a coffee filter, or a clean cloth. Let it cool down before you store it and you should add a pinch of salt for every quart of water.

However, boiling water in an emergency situation might not be possible, when this happens you can disinfect your water by using household bleach, but, not any old bleach, you must use unscented chlorine bleach. Do not use colored bleach or bleach that contains other cleaning agents; just regular bleach. It should only have between 6 to 8.25% of sodium hypochlorite. Another important thing to remember is that you only need a couple of drops per quart. You should have a dropper in your emergency kit for these situations. Once that is done, stir the water and let it stand for 30 minutes. At this point, the water should have a very light smell of chlorine, however, if it doesn't you should repeat the process and let it stand for 15 minutes. If the opposite happens and the water tastes too much like chlorine, you should add more water from your water source and wait a few hours until it dilutes.

For reference, here is the amount of bleach you should add depending on the volume of water:

- for one quart, add 2 drops if it's 6% or 8.25%
- for a gallon, add eight drops if it's 6%, or 6 drops if it's 8.25%

From here, just double every time the volume of water doubles.

You should note, however, that if your faucet uses municipal water, this already contains chlorine as well as other chemicals that enable it to be stored for a few months. In order to begin to store water, the first thing you need to do is to purchase cases of bottled water, if you look around for discounts you will find some at a fair price. This bottled water is essential for the first few days of an emergency, where everything is in a chaotic state and everyone is rushing to get resources, you will have the peace of mind of being able to drink bottled water. You will then have the time to focus on making more plans for the next few days. When preparing your supply of emergency water, hide it away out of sight, so the family doesn't go and use it every time they are looking for water. In an emergency situation, the water you have stored should only be used for cooking and drinking, for everything else, use water from other sources.

You may be wondering if that large swimming pool in your backyard would be a good source of water. You could use it for bathing but you can't consume it. Besides having higher levels of chlorine, there are also lots of other chemicals and stabilizers used in pool water. This is not good for drinking or cooking, however, for bathing and washing your clothes it's not a problem.

When it comes to wells, the situation is a little trickier. They contain water that you can drink and cook with and because they come with ready-made storage, they would be really handy to have around. However, in an emergency, when the power is out, it could be a problem. You need electricity to pump the water from a well into your home, so you would need the power to extract water from the well. However, there's still a solution; hand pumps. These can help bring water from wells into your faucets, with the only disadvantage being their cost, which is around $1,000. Although when it comes to surviving, that is a small price to pay. They are also fairly easy to install yourself.

If you have a gutter system in your home, you can collect rainwater. However, you need to place a barrel or some sort of container on the gutter downspout to collect it. If you don't have a gutter system, you should consider getting one, perhaps you can even install it yourself as without one, it's hard to catch rainwater efficiently. Remember, if you are using barrels, sometimes it might be hard to access the water so consider installing a spigot at the bottom of the barrel. You will still need to filter the water that collects the barrels, as it goes through roofing and will catch debris on the way down.

Wild water sources can be extremely useful in an emergency situation. These include lakes, rivers, ponds, or anything else that has running freshwater. In an emergency situation, you need to remember that you are probably not the only one that knows about a certain water source, so if you want to avoid any human contact, it is best to leave these as a last resort. Another thing to worry about is disinfecting the water you collect. Waterborne pathogens can be very dangerous, and they are usually found in wild water sources, regardless of how clean the water might seem.

If you are using natural water sources, you need to find a way to store the water and take it back to your refuge. Buckets are one option and you could bring a cart, or a wheelbarrow to transport them back to your house or shelter. If a cart or a wheelbarrow is out of the question, try a shoulder pole instead - it may require a little more effort but will help you bring that water buckets back to your shelter safely. Remember, when searching for wild sources of water, always look for running sources, such as rivers, these are less likely to have algae and other pathogens.

Filtration and Disinfection

You will need to filter and disinfect the water you collect from natural sources. Sometimes, the terms filtration and disinfection are used interchangeably, but they mean two different things. When you disinfect, you are killing pathogens or other viruses that may be in your water. When you filter it, you are removing parasites and larger debris that can be found in the water. Let's have a look at how we can do both in an emergency situation.

How should you go about filtering a bucket filled with dirty water from a wild source and turning it into drinkable water? Short answer: you have to build a filtration system. Start by using plastic bottles, ideally two-liter plastic ones. First, cut off the bottom of the bottles and place a coffee filter on it, make sure the lid is screwed on. Next, you will need to build the filter, which you can do using everyday materials, or stuff that you can easily get in DIY stores. First, place a small layer of activated charcoal, then add an inch or two of fine grain over the charcoal, and lastly, add gravel (the smaller the gravel the better) This should be enough to filter your water, but you can test it by adding coloring to the water and making it run down your DIY water filter, if the water comes out clean, it is well-filtered. This is an easy water filter to make as it only uses everyday items, however, you will need to change the filter regularly or every time the water runs slower than usual, or is not filtering properly.

Disinfection will allow us to kill off any bacteria or pathogens that may have passed through the filter. Boiling the water should be enough to safely drink the water. There is also another great disinfection method which uses ultraviolet rays.

To filter your water through solar disinfection, all you need to do is place the clear, bottled water in the sun. Make sure you remove any labeling on the bottle and that the bottle is clear and not colored. You still have to make sure the water is properly filtered before exposing it to the sunrays. If you have access to a rooftop, this might be an even better position to place your bottles of water. You should leave them in the sun for a whole day. If the sun is not shining brightly or the sky is cloudy, you should leave the bottles for two days. Alternatively, you can use UV disinfection products, these are portable devices and are usually battery-powered, or crank-powered. If you are using any of these devices, all you need is a short burst of UV light to disinfect your water. In an emergency situation, you should choose the crank-powered ones, so you don't have to rely on batteries. If all of these strategies fail, you can resort to calcium hypochlorite, or as it is best known, pool shock. However, look for 100% calcium hypochlorite and avoid anything that contains any other disinfectants. To disinfect the water with this, first, you need to add a teaspoon into two gallons of water, and then use a wooden spoon to stir it. Don't use a metal one, as this solution will corrode it. Once that solution is well mixed, add it to your water. Keep in mind, though, that the ratio here is one pint of the solution to twelve and a half gallons of the water you want to disinfect.

Water is probably the most important resource we need in an emergency. Being cautious and storing it beforehand can significantly increase our chances of survival in an emergency situation.

Searching for and Storing Food

After water, food is the most essential requirement a person has, but food can be even scarcer than water, especially if you think that is harder to stockpile than water is, and it doesn't fall from the sky either.

You could store large amounts of freeze-dried food, but having a diet solely comprised of that could make you ill, mainly because of the high quantities of sodium. Although it is not a bad plan to store some, it is hardly a solution to survive long term. Diversification of the food you store is essential to maintaining a balanced diet. In an emergency situation, there are three main sources of food; your own stores, growing food, and wild sources such as hunting or fishing. Let's see how we would go about each of these options.

Storing Food

While storing enough food to last for years might not be feasible for everyone, you should, at least, have some food reserves. When preparing your emergency plan, you should aim to have around three months of food stored. When you add other foods such as berries and vegetables or anything that you can grow, you can stretch your food storage to last for at least six months. This shouldn't be your first option when in an emergency, instead it should be a sort of a safety net if your most immediate sources of food don't work out.

When storing food, you should consider canned food, but also dry, or dried food such as pasta, grains and vegetables. Here are a few foods to consider when preparing your food reserves:

- Canned vegetables and fruits - These may not be as tasty as fresh ones but they still have the necessary nutrients and protein your body needs. They are extremely easy to store and last for at least a whole year.

- Rice - Store only white and brown rice, and be careful not to store long grain or any aromatic types of rice, as these have oils that can go bad.

- Beans – They are easy to store in cans, and are filled with protein. They are a great substitute for meat if you can't find any.

- Stews and soups - These are one of the easiest foods to make, and you can literally just add whatever food you have to hand and let it boil. This might be a great option in an emergency situation, and you can add flavor just by dropping a stock cube into it.

- Canned meat - Although not the best tasting food, it can be handy if hunting is not an option.

- Dry pasta - Dry pasta, when properly stored, can last for a very long time. Plus, it is easy to cook. It should be one of your top foods in your storage.

- Sprouts - These are very easy to grow and are high in proteins and nutrients. A great choice to have around, and they come in many varieties. In less than a week you can have them growing in your garden. All you need to do is rinse the seeds in water, and leave them in a jar overnight. The next day, drain the water and keep the seeds moist for three to five days, after which you will be able to harvest your sprouts.

- Cooking oils - In an emergency situation, the best oils to store are olive and vegetable oil, as they last for longer. Don't forget to use oils as they have essential fats that your body needs to work properly.

- Herbs and spices - These are probably not that important in terms of the nutrients they can provide your body, but they are essential to make any food taste good. Plus, in their dry form, they are easy to store.

Growing Food

Our gardens can provide us with great sources of food and we should take full advantage of them. Growing food takes time and, in an emergency, it will certainly be hard to acquire any seeds from the store, so it is best to be prepared.

But in times of peace, the store is the best place to find seeds for growing vegetables, in fact, you can also harvest the seeds from the fruits and vegetables that you grow in order to grow more.

Planning how to grow food is a time-consuming process, however, it is essential if you want to have access to an array of different fruits and vegetables. You can start by listing vegetables that you and your family usually eat. Then, you will need to understand what type of crops grow well in the area you live in, as well as the times it takes to grow each crop and how to grow them properly. You should stock up on those seeds and if you can, you should start growing your little garden straight away and not wait for it to be too late. Having the necessary experience in an emergency situation can be extremely helpful.

Raising Animals

Raising animals is something that you should also consider as having a diverse diet is very important, even more so in an emergency situation. Things like chickens, rabbits, sheep, and goats are easier to get and take care of. There are many classes, both online and offline that can teach you how to raise farm animals, but you should opt for offline courses as you will probably get more practical experience that way.

If you want something more than just meat, and you have the possibility, consider raising tilapia fish. These fish are easy to breed, and grow fast, all you need is a small pond and food for them.

Foraging

Wild edibles can be found virtually anywhere. Foraging helped early humans to survive, so it can certainly help us too in an emergency situation.

You should be able to find various courses on foraging wild edibles. Local classes are great because they will teach you about the edibles you might find in your particular area. It is also really important to know which types of plants you will find in which season. One great way to get familiar with the edibles in your area is to go for walks, or hikes, and practice identifying plants. You have to remember that some of the berries and plants you find can be dangerous and eating them could have serious health implications. It is therefore essential to know which ones are safe to eat and which ones are not. Eating plants that are not safe will only cause you more problems.

Fishing, Hunting, and Trapping

Before a disaster situation strikes you should learn how to fish, hunt, and trap wild animals and understand how many times you should do so in order to maintain a healthy balance of ingredients.

For those of you that live in a city or suburbs, this might be a little more complicated, mainly because of the scarcity of animals, as well as the number of hunters out there. With that said, hitting the trail and searching for wild animals to hunt shouldn't be your primary way of obtaining food. Note that, some of the techniques explained in the following section, might not be legal where you live. However, many of these laws might not be binding if society falls and we need to fight for our own survival. With that said, if you want to practice your hunting and fishing skills in times of peace, do so, within the law.

Fishing

When fishing for survival, automatic fishing reels and trotlines can help you increase your catches. A trotline is a heavy line that has smaller ones hanging from it, allowing you to have more lines in the water and thus a greater chance of capturing more fish. It is easier to fish using trotlines in rivers and smaller streams where water runs, rather than in more static waters such as lakes. A rope or a larger cord, is placed across a river's banks, and in between those, you have smaller threads of fish lines called snoods. Because each snood has a hook, the odds of success increase exponentially. There are a few things that you need to know when fishing with trotlines, such as the precise space between snoods. You need to leave some space between the smaller lines, to stop them from getting tangled together. Another great advantage of fishing with a trotline is that you don't necessarily need to be holding the rod, you can leave it and come back and check it a few times a day, to retrieve fish and to free more hooks. However, this might not be the best option if you don't have the river or the stream to yourself, as other people might come and steal your hard-caught fish.

With automatic reels, you have more freedom to do other things while you are fishing. You will find them in most fishing and hunting shops, and they will certainly be of great help if you find yourself in survival mode. All you need to do is drop the hook with the bait into the water and attach the reel to something heavy like a tree trunk or a rock. The struggling of the fish, when hooked, will activate the reel to pull out of the water and retract the line.

But of course, it is not as simple as finding a river and going fishing. You need to know where to fish, and if the fish population around your area is healthy enough to keep producing fish for the long term. Knowing the species that live in the lake or river will also help you find the best way to capture the fish.

Trapping

Traps are a great way to acquire wild meat, mainly because you won't need to be present at all times, you just need to set up the trap and come and check on it once in a while to see if you have caught something. In fact, if this is going to be your way of obtaining wild meat, you should set quite a few and check them at least once every day. However, you don't want to spend too much time in the same place setting up traps or constantly checking if they have caught anything, as this might frighten the very creatures you want to capture.

There are many varieties of snares and other traps that are easy to set up. However, understanding how to properly use a snare, takes some practice. It is good to understand what type of animals you can trap in your area, so you can set up the right size of snares, and know where to place them.

Hunting

Your ability to hunt for wild meat really depends on your skill and experience. Usually, people hunt using firearms or bows. You need to know the population of wild animals in your area, as well as what species live there. If it is mainly big game, such as deer, you might be better off by hunting, however, if the local wildlife population is more based on smaller animals such as rabbits, or foxes then trapping might be easier for you to put food on the table.

Hygiene

Personal hygiene will be one of those things that will deteriorate the longer you are in survival mode. Scarcity of hygiene products, and lack of sewer line cleaning, will make your hygiene harder to maintain. The good news is that your body, or in particular, your nose, will get used to it rather quickly. Let us go through the different sections of hygiene and ways to mitigate certain issues.

Toilet Facilities

If you stay indoors, in a home, or any other place with a toilet, in the short term, you will have no problem flushing after you have used it. Flushes can still be used even without power; all you need to do is manually fill the tank. However, this will stop working once sewer lines stop being cleaned and the waste has nowhere to go. You should plan for such an event.

Although chemical toilets can be a potential solution, they might also not work in the long term, as you would have to store large amounts of whatever chemical you use to treat the waste. That leaves us with much simpler solutions, first up: buckets. You can find and purchase buckets at any hardware store. If you get a five-gallon bucket or bigger, you can add your own toilet seat, which will end up being a relative luxury. In the bottom of the bucket, you will need to add some sand and keep the source of sand nearby with a scoop, so you can cover the waste. If you have baking soda or laundry detergent, you can add a little over it, but you are probably better off if you save those for other things. Ideally, every member of your family or group should have their own bucket, and once it is half full, you need to throw the waste away, or it might get too full to move it around. If buckets and sand are not a viable option, heavy-duty bags can do the trick, however, these need to be emptied more often because you don't want to have the bag burst open when you are trying to move it.

Alternatively, you can dig a hole or a latrine, but this requires significantly more work. Although if you do choose to dig a latrine, make sure you dig it wide enough (about two or three feet), and deep enough (also two or three feet). After you have used it, cover the waste with a scoop of earth or dirt.

Toilet paper won't last forever, so you will eventually need to think about a solution for that problem. Magazines and newspapers are a great solution, but old clothes, such as t-shirts, or socks will work better in the long term, as you can wash them. It is always important to wash your hands after you have used the toilet, but in survival situations like this, it is essential. Whether you use sanitizer or wash your hands in a river, it is important that you do it. If you are using sanitizer, remember that you will have alcohol in your hands, at least straight after you have used it, don't go near open flames or any other flammable components or you might catch fire.

Laundry

This is one of those things that you might only remember to do after a week or so into an emergency situation, but in the long term can be quite important. Planning for it is just as essential as anything else, and with the right preparation, you can set yourself up well.

Hand washing your clothes can be both time and energy-consuming. However, you can make it easier by purchasing a large tub, a smaller tub, and a washboard. Fill up the large tub with water and detergent, ideally a biodegradable one, and scrub. Place the washed clothes in a smaller tub with just water and hang them out to dry. It may be that you can't get hold of a washboard, if that is the case, you need to scrub them with your hands, slap them against a large rock, or anything hard and not particularly dirty, although this is less efficient.

You could achieve the same results with a large bucket, a lid, and a plunger. Make a hole in the lid, just large enough for the handle of the plunger to fit in, add water, and detergent and use the plunger to clean your clothes. You should use a little scrubbing brush just to take out the more stubborn stains.

Showering and Bathing

The best thing you can do when it comes to being able to maintain personal hygiene is to purchase a camp shower. They are easy to transport and hang on a tree branch. All you need to do is fill the camp shower bag with water and leave it to be heated up by the sun, although don't expect it to be as hot as a regular shower. These camp shower bags come with a nozzle and a hose like a sort of showerhead. Ideally, you would have a large container which you would stand in so you can catch as much of the water as possible and reuse it for other things.

If you can't get a camp shower, then, the next best thing is to have someone pour water from a bucket over you. It might be slightly more primitive, but it is just as efficient.

If you are in a situation where water is rather scarce and it is impossible to take showers, a sponge bath is your next solution. You can clean yourself that way, it takes a little longer, but it also requires a lot less water. With roughly two cups of water, you can have a sponge bath.

Save and stock up shampoo and soap. However, you don't need expensive stuff and every soap and shampoo will do pretty much the same thing.

Tooth Care

Taking care of your teeth is important in an emergency situation where you can't go to a dentist. A bad toothache can be very painful and stop you from doing your regular daily activities, which can translate into a lack of food and other necessities. Toothbrushes are cheap, so you can stash quite a few of them, when it comes to toothpaste, that can be quite tricky to get and you may eventually run out. In that eventuality, you can add salt and baking soda together to make a fairly effective toothpaste. You will need two parts baking soda to one part salt. You won't feel as fresh as after using regular toothpaste, but it will do the trick. Remember to also stockpile some dental floss and mouthwash as these will be essential for your oral hygiene. If you run out of mouthwash, you can make a primitive one with equal parts water and hydrogen peroxide.

The main objective here is to avoid developing cavities, abscesses, and other issues that can be really painful, or even life-threatening if they are not properly treated.

Waste Disposal

We need to be able to dispose of all the waste that we generate. In today's society, its easy, all we do is place all of our waste into our garbage cans and every week or so, someone comes and picks it up. However, it poses a much bigger problem when you are in survival mode.

Let's start with general garbage. This is waste that people generate through food, packaging, or anything else that does not come out of our bodies. Families, in particular, can generate quite a lot of garbage. In an emergency situation, you should look at burning some of it, but also try to reuse any of it if you can. Plastic containers and tin cans, can be turned into vases for plants, or form part of an alarm system. The more creative you get, the less garbage you have to dispose of. If you can't burn the rest, then the next solution would be to bury it somewhere far from your location. Also, don't bury it close to a source of water, or your own crops as waste may become contaminated.

Human waste is a different type of waste and can actually be used for quite a few things. If you choose to dispose of it, you can bury it, but remember to do it far from water sources. Ideally, you would be digging a latrine and filling it up. Once it is about two feet from the top, bury it for good and start a new one. You can also burn it, but you need to let it dry for a couple of days, which can intensify the smell of it. You could also add flammable liquid to it in order to make it easier to burn. However, this is far from the best solution. Burying it is far better.

However, you should use some of the waste as fertilizer for your garden. This can be great to grow crops faster and healthier. Although if you are doing that, you will need to keep urine and feces separate. For this, it is best to use a funnel to direct the urine into a jug or a bucket.

To use urine in your garden, you need to let it age for a couple of months, then mix it with dirty water from your laundry for example. The mix here should be one part urine and eight parts water and then added the mix straight into the garden.

The feces should be collected separately into a bucket, when that is full add a lid with a hole. You would have to let it sit for about a year before you could use it for composting. This is really a long-term situation, and you should still do it even if you don't think the emergency will last that long because it is better to be prepared. We will talk more about how to use waste in your garden in another chapter.

Keeping Warm

Clothing and shelter are two basic necessities, depending on the weather where you are you could last a little longer without either, but in the long term, you wouldn't survive being exposed so much.

Ideally, your home would still be standing and even without power or water, it would still be the best shelter. If your home was destroyed or somehow unavailable to live in, the next best thing would be a family member's house or a friend's house. The important thing is having a roof over your head and clothes to warm you up or protect you from the sun.

Clothing

Clothing should be a priority as it is your first defense against the weather. Even though many of us have entire wardrobes and closets filled with all types of clothes, bringing them with you in the eventuality that you need to leave your home might not be the most practical thing.

In cases like this, you need to pick a few clothes. You would need to prepare some clothes in advance as much of the clothes we wear today would end up being too impractical and would offer very little protection in an emergency situation. When packing clothes for an emergency, you should prioritize comfort, practicality, and durability over fashion and style. Although this seems logical, most people have never been in an emergency situation and would probably pick their favorite clothes rather than thinking logically.

The best shoes to wear in a survival situation are comfortable ones. Thick socks will also help you protect against cold, water, and other dangers in the wild. You should go for high quality here, as the discounted socks people usually buy would not last very long with constant washing and use. Having thick and comfortable work boots is also a great option. Thick soles and ankle support is what you should be looking for. Packing a pair of sneakers when the weather is warmer is prudent, especially as you may need to walk quite a bit. If you live in an area where it snows quite frequently, get a pair of snow boots too.

Pants are also essential. You will need some robust jeans which are comfortable for both walking and working in. These may be harder to hand wash and will take quite a long time to dry. Alternatively, cargo pants made out of cotton are a fantastic option; besides being comfortable, they usually have lots of pockets that will come in handy. A few pairs of shorts for when it's warmer outside should also be part of your emergency closet. You don't want them to be too short though, as they won't protect your legs as much. Add in a couple of belts, even if you don't need them to secure your pants in place as they can be extremely useful in other situations.

When it comes to tops, choose ones which are durable and comfortable over fashionable. You should add t-shirts, button-down shirts, flannel shirts, long sleeve shirts and sweatshirts.

Although underwear is not as essential as the items of clothing we have mentioned so far, it is still something that you want to have in an emergency. Underwear will help prevent sweat getting to certain body parts such as groins, and are really easy to wash and dry. You want to wear the same underwear for at least two weeks before you wash them, otherwise, you will be spending way too much time washing clothes and too little on other important activities.

Outerwear such as heavy coats certainly has a place in your emergency closet. Especially if you live in an area where it rains or snows quite frequently. In fact, the head is where we lose most of our heat, so keeping it covered with a hood or a hat can keep us warmer for longer.

You will need a pair of gloves that keep your hands warm but which allow you to maintain maximum dexterity in your fingers. You should also add in a rain poncho, these are cheap and can protect you from the rain, they are also easily foldable and light, so won't occupy much space. Having a good quality parka for more severe winters can really help you get through the harsher months. If possible, pick one where you can remove the liner so you can make it warmer or cooler depending on the weather situation you are in. These are not that cheap but are essential if you live in extremely cold places.

It is important, especially when it is cold outside, to dress in layers. Particularly if you are doing chores or physical tasks. You don't want to get too hot and sweat over all your clothes especially if you take breaks and that sweat turns cold. With layers, you can easily remove and add clothes and manage your body temperature a lot better to avoid getting too sweaty. Something else to consider when preparing for an emergency is whether or not to pack camouflage clothes. Although this can be great if you are out hunting, providing you have the right camouflage for the environment you are in, most people live in suburbia, and this means that your camouflage won't particularly help you. Just keep this in mind when picking out your clothes.

For Spring and Summer months:

- shirts, loose-fitting
- comfortable and durable shorts
- hat

For Fall and Winter months:

- long sleeve shirts
- gloves
- boots/ snow boots
- heavy coat
- sneakers
- jacket
- thick socks
- knit hat
- other shirts (ideally flannel)

Shelter

Ideally, your home will be your shelter as it already has everything you need, even if you end up with no power. Keep in mind that you should avoid lighting fires inside the house. Electrical heaters and other forms of heat that we are used to, won't be working, and the risk of setting fire to your house is higher since smoke detectors will eventually run out of battery and the fire department will certainly not be operational. But to ensure both fire alarms and smoke detectors are still working, make sure they are in good condition, at least every month. Place them near the kitchen, if you usually cook there and near your bedrooms, in case a fire starts during the night.

Having a fire extinguisher in easy-to-grab locations is also essential. If you don't have access to one, baking soda can also help you put out fires. Remember, if a fire has started while you are cooking, don't add water to put it out, because that fire probably is being fueled with grease which can easily spatter everywhere and spread the fire. Also remember when you are cooking with fire, having good ventilation is key, so you and your family don't suffer from carbon monoxide poisoning.

But how do you keep yourself and your family warm if you can't light a fire? Ideally, you and your family would be spread between one or two rooms maximum. If, for example, you live in a house with two floors, you should try to close off the upper floor so the heat remains on the first floor where you are. The more blankets you have the better, of course, and the more people under one or two blankets the more heat you can retain. If you have access to fire-safe bricks, you can do a little trick by heating them up and wrapping them in towels or clothes under the blankets you are using. If you don't have fire-safe bricks, don't use regular bricks as these will likely break. Instead use large rocks.

However, there are situations where the cold won't be an issue, and instead, the heat might. How do you cool off in high temperatures when the air conditioning is not working? Well, the first thing to do to keep your body temperature down is to do all the necessary chores early in the morning, or later in the afternoon when the sun is not as hot. If possible, don't do tasks under the intense sun. If you have to, remember to take breaks to cool off, drink water, and, if you can, work under a shade. Remember to use light-colored clothes as these retain the heat a lot less than darker hues. The thinner the fabrics the better: usually cotton will do just fine under extreme heat. Having a hat, or a scarf around your head can help you keep the heat off your face; a wide-brimmed hat would be better as it would also cover your neck.

At home, keeping the interior at a reasonable temperature and as cool as you can is essential. The heat can have consequences on your sleep and how you rest, and we need a good night's sleep to stay healthy. Having curtains and drapes closed during the day will help keep the inside of the house cool. It is also important to keep the windows closed during the day and during the hours of extreme heat, only open them in the early morning or in the evening to let the cool air come in. If you have multiple windows, you can open them all to create cross ventilation and air out your shelter faster and more effectively. Insulated walls can be great to keep the cool air from leaving the house. If you don't already have that in your home, you should think about investing in it. Having insulated walls can also keep you warmer in the winter.

Planting trees on the west and east side of your property can also offer shade during the hotter months. However, this takes quite a long time, depending on the tree, and you need to keep them healthy, as a dead or dying tree can be a danger to your house.

Power and Electricity

In the long run, preparing for a power outage is redundant. However, you should still plan to have some electronics working in the first few days of a long-term catastrophe. And if you are thinking that solar panels might save you when the power goes out, they won't. These will also become useless when the rest of the power is cut off for safety measures. Plus installing one can be quite expensive, even though there are a few government programs that can help you, in long-term survival it seems a waste of money (in any normal circumstance, solar panels are great for the environment and save you a lot of money in the long term).

The first thing you should do is assemble an emergency preparedness kit that includes supplies for both short and medium-term power outages. Having a generator can help you in the short term, but because they usually need fuel such as gasoline, or something similar, it would be hard to maintain them for a long time. In your emergency kit, you should have a couple of flashlights, lanterns, and a few extra batteries for radios, although if you can have crank-powered radio and flashlights, even better, as these can last you for a long time.

Unplugging your electronics will keep you protected from temporary surges, and protect your electronics too. If you do have a generator and fuel to make it work, use it sparingly so as to extend its lifespan. Also, you should always use a generator outside your house, if you don't know the wattage of your generator or the appliances you then refrain from using a generator at all, as this might break both devices.

Candles are fair game, and probably one of the best sources of light at night, but you have to be very careful with them, a little slip and your house could catch on fire. Always use candles away from flammable objects like gas, wood, or curtains.

The usual gas generators won't cut it in a long-term survival situation. They are impossible to mask, which means sooner or later someone will know you are using one and either steal it or simply leverage it to get something in exchange, or you will inevitably run out of fuel for it. Saying that power generators are great as a short-term solution.

However, portable solar generators can be a great alternative. These come in many shapes and forms, but usually are portable solar panels with inputs so you can use any device you want. Another product that might come in handy is a Biolite camp stove, this device converts heat into electricity, all you need to do is start a fire on the stove and the device will convert the energy for you through a USB port. Although with this device you can only charge something that is USB connected, you can be cooking while you do it. There is a myriad of other devices that can do that, you just need to search for one that suits your needs. Although even with all of this, you should be prepared to live a life with no electricity, and it is totally doable, humanity did that for thousands of years, even though it might be quite harsh at first.

Emergencies can come in many forms, famine, pandemics, economic collapse, or even war or terrorism. We need to be prepared for any of these scenarios. We need to adapt to these circumstances as quickly as we possibly can and find the best way to survive. In recent years, we have seen many of these catastrophes happening and although many didn't bring the world to its knees, many people suffered. The day may arrive when our governments will not be able to keep order and we are in a situation where survival of the fittest will happen.

One of the first things that you should look into is having a plan to search for water if you don't have pre-established reserves. The human body will not survive more than two or three days without water, so knowing where to look for it, how to treat it and disinfect it, and also how to store it is important for your survival. After that, food should be your primary concern. If you have planned for such catastrophes, you should have a good stockpile of goods, however, these should not be your primary source of food, but instead a reserve for when you don't have fresh food. When it comes to food procurement, hunting, fishing, trapping, and foraging should be your main activities. Learning how to do all of these things can help you survive for longer periods and put food on the table for you and your family. Knowing how to store your fresh food is also something that you should learn, as well as raising animals for food.

Hygiene might not be one of your main priorities in the first few days of a catastrophe, however, you should plan for it too, especially since a disaster situation can drag on for a long time. Simple things like waste disposal and germs can become serious issues if you don't take the necessary measures. Another thing that you should take into consideration is your clothing. This should be prepared according to the climate you are in. Plan what clothes are most important and put everything else to good use by making improvised bandages and other things that you might need. If you need to evacuate, you will only be able to take only a few pieces of clothing with you, so make sure you have that planned beforehand too.

Book 2

Surviving 7 Years with Rice and Beans

Introduction

When it comes to emergency preparedness, most people think about canned goods and what they might need for a few days or weeks, but how about an entire month's worth of food with just one simple - and cheap - cooking staple? Rice will make up the bulk of your preparedness diet. It can be cooked in rice cookers and lasts for up to 30 days. You should also consider adding beans, nuts and lentils (with their own cooking times) to round out your menu.

While a 30-day supply of rice may not seem like much, it's a good base to have on-hand. You can incorporate grains and legumes into the recipes that you enjoy from your go-to cookbook or ones that you find online. You might even pick up a new recipe or two from friends, relatives or your local community.

All of your favorite foods can be prepared with rice, beans, lentils and other grains as the main ingredient. Rice takes different amounts of time to cook depending on how it's been milled (whole grain is healthier). Most recipes require that you wash the grains prior to cooking. You can do this by filling a pot with two inches of water and bringing it to a boil. Place the grains into a strainer and boil them for about 20-25 minutes. When they are soft you can drain them.

Rice cookers have a number of benefits that you would not want to miss out on in an emergency situation. They can be bought for less than $100 and they make cooking rice really convenient. They can also be used to prepare other quick meals, such as porridge and pasta, which can be difficult for some to cook by hand.

When you're ready to cook, put the rice and water in the cooker and let it boil. Then cook it until all the water is gone.

You can add ingredients like beans and lentils on top of your rice or incorporate elements from other recipes. You can measure out the grains, beans and lentils into one-cup portions that will keep them separate until they are needed (you might want to add some vinegar in between to help keep them fresh). Some people like to keep a large container full of toppings (vegetables, nuts, seeds) that can be prepared at any time you choose. Some great options for storing this kind of food include using either canning jars or food-storage totes, which can be purchased in sets of four at Walmart.

In an emergency situation, you will need to find a way to eat the meals you have prepared in advance. Rice cookers are perfect for the job because you can use them to cook mushrooms and other vegetables, on top of rice and beans.

Rice is easy to prepare and you don't have to worry too much about cooking times (although it's important that you cook the right amount). It also offers the added benefit of being so filling.

Soybeans, lentils and other beans can be cooked with rice, beans and grains to make delicious side dishes to accompany your main course.

You can use a large food-storage container or two smaller ones (such as glass jam jars) to store this sort of food. The same tips apply if you choose to store nuts and seeds, which are high in protein and can provide you with a quick snack when the need arises.

Boiled rice can be easily stored in any food storage container. Just add an airtight lid or use a vacuum sealer to make sure the rice stays fresh for as long as possible. You can also divide the rice into smaller portions so it will be easy to store and not take up a lot of space.

If you find your current food storage running low because of short expiration dates, don't give up hope just yet: if properly stored, dried rice has been known to last as long as 20 years and sometimes even longer!

Chapter 1: Beans and Rice, the Best Survival Food

Beans and rice, two of the world's most popular staples. Beans provide protein from plants, and rice provides your body with lots of energy. Combined with herbs and spices, beans are a good source of vitamins like folate, thiamin, niacin and riboflavin. They also contain important minerals such as iron. The carbs in these legumes give you important energy boosts too!

This book is all about the importance of beans in survival food since they can make any meal more satisfying without having to spend too much time cooking or searching for ingredients that may not be available during an emergency situation. I have worked with beans in cooking over the years, mostly because of the texture and taste they give to stews, soups and other dishes. The ones that I use the most are black beans and kidney beans, but there are many other fantastic ones to choose from.

Beans must be soaked before cooking because they contain lectins or proteins that make them harder to digest. A simple way to get rid of these proteins is by soaking them overnight using plenty of water. Also, you should remove the hulls before boiling them for about five hours because these are hard to digest too. The longer you cook the beans, the better the quality of your meal.

Rice is another food that can be prepared in a survival situation because it is commonly available and easy to use. However, it needs to be kept dry because it tends to stick together if it gets wet. It is important to clean the rice before cooking by washing off the impurities and letting it soak overnight because this will give you a better texture in the final dish. You can boil or steam your rice, but I prefer doing both with a pressure cooker as this reduces cooking time.

Benefits of Beans and Rice

Beans and rice are an excellent source of protein, fiber, minerals, and antioxidants. Potatoes are a good source of potassium and are a great complement to beans. Beans provide fiber and other nutrients important for digestive health while rice is an excellent source of carbohydrates.

By combining these two easy-to-find foods into one dish you can create a complete meal full of nutrients that will leave you feeling satisfied and you won't need to prepare anything else on the side. By adding some green vegetables such as broccoli, a small amount of dried or fresh herbs such as parsley, mint, dill or basil and some low-fat cheese, you can really elevate the flavor of a simple rice and beans dish.

If you're looking for a healthy and affordable way to pack in the protein, beans and rice are your best bet. Not only do they make a high-quality substitute for meat when you want to cut down on costs, but they also deliver exceptional nutritional value.

Beans are a complete protein source, meaning they offer all nine essential amino acids that our bodies need but can't produce themselves — an amazing feat considering it's usually really hard to find this spectrum of amino acids in plant-based foods! This means beans can give vegetarians an incredibly reliable way of getting their daily protein requirements met without resorting to animal sources.

Brown rice is also a complete protein source and it offers more fiber and B vitamins than white rice. As an added bonus, beans and rice are both very cost effective — especially when purchased in bulk — making them a widely accessible way to get the nutrition your body needs.

Now let's look at the ways beans and brown rice can benefit your health:

High in Fiber: Both beans and rice offer roughly 6 grams of dietary fiber per cup, which means you're getting a satisfyingly large dose of this important nutrient every time you eat a dish that contains them. Beans are particularly good for fiber intake due to their high fiber content and complex carbs that make it easily digested.

High in Vitamin E: Not only do brown rice and beans contain significant levels of beta-carotene, they also boast some impressive levels of vitamin E. Brown rice and beans both have around 9 milligrams of vitamin E per cup, which is pretty "healthy" for a plant-based food!

Contribute to Healthy Digestion: Beans are an excellent source of prebiotics. When consumed in the right amount, prebiotics can help stimulate healthy gut function. When prebiotics reach the large intestine, they help facilitate the growth of beneficial bacteria that make for a healthy digestive tract.

Beans are an excellent source of prebiotics: When consumed in the right amount, prebiotics can help stimulate healthy gut function. When prebiotics reach the large intestine, they help facilitate the growth of beneficial bacteria that make for a healthy digestive tract.

Provide Protein You Need: Beans and rice are a great way to include protein in your diet without resorting to meat or other animal-derived foods, because both are nutrient-dense sources of complete protein (each one contains all 9 essential amino acids).

An Excellent Alternative to Meat: Beans and rice have a nice flavor that makes it easy to replace animal protein sources with these more nutritious ingredients. Even better, they're highly affordable ingredients that you can purchase in bulk, which makes them very cost effective.

Nutritional Information for Beans and Rice:

Cooked beans contain about 14 grams of protein per cup. A 3/4 cup portion of cooked brown rice contains about 5 grams of protein.

One cup of cooked beans or 1/2 cup of raw beans has an excellent source of folate. Brown rice is an excellent source of magnesium and iron, as well as being a good source of B vitamins.

Beans and brown rice are also great sources of fiber, calcium, iron and vitamin E.

Beans and brown rice have a good amount of thiamin and niacin. A cup has about 4 milligrams of thiamin (vitamin B1). Brown rice contains about 4 milligrams niacin (vitamin B3), which is an essential nutrient for the metabolism of fats in the body.

Beans and brown rice are good sources of iron. One cup of cooked beans contains about 3 milligrams of iron, while a cup of brown rice has 1 milligram.

Beans have about 27 milligrams of magnesium per cup, which is about 9 percent of the Recommended Daily Allowance for magnesium (400 mg daily). Brown rice has about 46 milligrams per cup, which is approximately 16 percent of the RDA. Magnesium is a mineral that plays an important role in bone development and protein synthesis.

Brown rice and beans are both good sources of manganese, with a cup containing over half the RDA (1.7 milligrams). Manganese is a mineral involved in DNA synthesis, protein and fat metabolism.

Beans are a good source of copper and potassium, with one cup providing about eight percent of the RDA for each one. One cup of cooked brown rice contains about 3 milligrams of copper and 1.5 milligrams of potassium. Potassium is an electrolyte found in plants that allows the muscles to contract and helps control the muscle cells' nerves. Copper is involved in bone health, oxygen transportation and brain function.

Beans have high levels of folate (about 40 percent daily recommended amount). Folate is a B vitamin that helps produce red blood cells and plays an important role in DNA synthesis.

Beans have high levels of manganese. A cup has over half the RDA. Manganese is a mineral involved in DNA synthesis, protein and fat metabolism.

Beans and rice are both good sources of copper and potassium, with one cup providing about eight percent of the RDA for each one.

Chapter 2: Lunch

Black Bean Mushroom Fettuccine

Preparation time: 5 minutes
Cooking time: 5 minutes
Servings: 6

Ingredients
- 9 ounces whole-wheat fettuccine
- 1 tablespoon olive oil
- 1 ¾ cups baby Portobello mushrooms, sliced
- 1 garlic clove, minced
- 1 (14.5-ounce) can diced tomatoes with their juices
- 1 (15-ounce) can black beans, drained and rinsed; or 5 ounces dry black beans, soaked and cooked
- 1 teaspoon dried rosemary
- ½ teaspoon dried oregano
- 2 cups baby spinach

Directions
1. Cook the pasta per the package's directions. Drain and set aside.
2. In a large skillet, heat oil over medium heat.
3. Add the mushrooms and cook until tender, about 4-6 minutes.
4. Add the garlic and cook until fragrant, about 1 minute.
5. Add the tomatoes, beans, rosemary, and oregano. Cook until evenly heated, about 1 minute.
6. Add the spinach and cook until wilted, about 2 minutes.
7. Add in the cooked pasta and toss to combine well.
8. Serve warm.

Nutrition:
Calories: 255, fat: 3 g, carbs: 45g, protein: 12g, sodium: 23g

White Bean Shrimp Spaghetti

Preparation time: 5 minutes
Cooking time: 20-25 minutes
Servings: 4

Ingredients
- 8 ounces whole-wheat spaghetti
- Kosher salt, to taste

- Freshly ground black pepper, to taste
- ¼ cup extra-virgin olive oil
- 1 shallot, chopped
- 1 (14-ounce) can white beans, drained and rinsed; or 5 ounces dry white beans, soaked and cooked
- 3 jarred cherry peppers or pepperoncini, roughly chopped
- 2 cloves garlic, chopped
- ¼-½ teaspoon crushed red pepper flakes
- ¾ pound medium shrimp, peeled and deveined
- ½ cup dry white wine
- Juice and zest of ½ lemon
- ½ cup flat-leaf parsley, roughly chopped

Directions
1. Cook the pasta per the package's directions. Reserve ⅔ cup of the pasta water, then drain and set aside.
2. In a medium saucepan or skillet, heat oil over medium heat.
3. Add the shallot and cook until softened and translucent, about 2 minutes.
4. Add the cherry peppers/pepperoncini, beans, garlic, crushed red pepper flakes, and ½ teaspoon of kosher salt. Continue to cook until garlic is mildly browned, about 2-3 minutes.
5. Mix in the shrimp and cook for 3 minutes or until opaque.
6. Add in the wine and cook for 2 minutes.
7. Add the lemon zest and pasta. Toss well to combine.
8. Add the pasta water, freshly ground black pepper, kosher salt, and parsley.
9. Stir gently and serve warm.

Nutrition: Calories 470, fat: 17g, carbs: 67g, protein: 19g, sodium: 91g

Parmesan Tuscan Bean Pasta

Preparation time: 10 minutes
Cooking time: 20 minutes
Servings: 4

Ingredients
- 8 ounces linguine or fettuccine pasta
- 1 tablespoon olive oil
- 1 tablespoon unsalted butter
- 3 cloves garlic, minced
- 1 pint cherry or grape tomatoes
- 10 cranks freshly ground black pepper
- ½ teaspoon kosher salt
- ½ teaspoon dried basil

- 1 (15-ounce) can cannellini beans, drained and rinsed; or 5 ounces dry cannellini beans, soaked and cooked
- 4 ounces baby spinach
- 3 ounces parmesan cheese, shredded

Directions
1. Cook the pasta per the package's directions. Drain and set aside.
2. In a large skillet, heat butter and olive oil over medium heat.
3. Add the garlic and cook until fragrant, about one minute.
4. Add the tomatoes, freshly ground black pepper, kosher salt, and basil. Cook until the tomatoes start to release their juices and their skin bursts.
5. Mix in the spinach and cook until wilted, about 2 minutes.
6. Add the beans and cook until heated for about 2 minutes.
7. Add more kosher salt to taste, then add the pasta and stir to coat evenly with the sauce.
8. Top with the shredded parmesan and serve warm.

Nutrition:
Calories: 556, fat: 13.5g, carbs: 81g, protein: 28.5 g, sodium: 11g

Anchovy White Bean Pasta

Preparation time: 15 minutes
Cooking time: 25 minutes
Servings: 4-6

Ingredients
- 4 tablespoons olive oil
- 4 medium cloves garlic, minced
- 4 anchovy filets, minced
- 1 teaspoon crushed red pepper flakes
- 2 (15.5-ounce) cans white beans or cannellini beans, drained and rinsed; or 10 ounces dry white/cannellini beans, soaked and cooked
- 1 ⅓ cups low-sodium vegetable stock
- 1 splash heavy cream, optional
- Pinch of freshly ground black pepper and kosher salt, or to taste
- 1 pound orecchiette, penne, or tubular pasta of your choice
- 1½ pounds broccoli rabe, trimmed and cut into 1½-inch pieces
- Juice of ½ lemon
- ½ cup ricotta cheese, optional
- ½ cup parmesan cheese, grated, optional

Direction
1. In a medium saucepan or skillet, heat oil over medium-low heat.
2. Add the garlic, anchovy filets, and crushed red pepper flakes. Cook until the anchovies disintegrate, about 1-2 minutes.

3. Add the stock, beans, and heavy cream (if using).
4. Simmer for 4-5 minutes or until the mixture thickens. Gently smash the beans to make them half-mushy.
5. Remove from heat, then season with freshly ground black pepper and kosher salt, to taste.
6. Cook the pasta per the package's directions. Reserve ⅓ cup of the pasta water, then drain and set aside.
7. In boiling water, cook the broccoli until wilted, about 3-4 minutes. Drain and set aside.
8. In a large deep saucepan, add the broccoli, pasta, and reserved pasta water. Simmer for 1 minute over low heat.
9. Season to taste with freshly ground black pepper and kosher salt. Mix in the lemon juice and a few dollops of ricotta cheese, if desired.
10. Top with the parmesan cheese and crushed red pepper flakes, then serve.

Nutrition:
Calories: 584, fat: 22g, carbs: 67g, protein: 27g, sodium: 15g

Broccoli Navy Bean Pasta

Preparation time: 15-20 minutes
Cooking time: 20 minutes
Servings: 8

Ingredients
- 1 lb. whole-wheat spaghetti
- 12 garlic cloves, peeled and thinly sliced
- 3 cups canned navy beans, drained and rinsed; or 1 cup dry navy beans, soaked and cooked
- 1 head broccoli, cut into slim florets
- 1 medium onion, sliced
- Juice of 1 lemon
- 1 teaspoon crushed red pepper flakes
- Freshly ground black pepper and kosher salt, to taste
- 1 tablespoon extra-virgin olive oil
- 1 packed cup flat-leaf parsley, minced

Directions
1. Cook pasta per the package's directions. Drain the water and set the cooked pasta aside, reserving ½ cup of the pasta water.
2. In a medium saucepan or skillet, heat oil over medium heat.
3. Add the onion, garlic, freshly ground black pepper and kosher salt. Cook until the onion is softened and translucent, about 7-8 minutes.
4. Add the crushed red pepper flakes and broccoli florets. Cook for 5 minutes or until the broccoli becomes slightly tender.

5. Add the pasta, freshly ground black pepper, and kosher salt to taste. Add the reserved pasta water and stir to combine.
6. Add the lemon juice and parsley, then serve warm.

Nutrition:
Calories: 328, fat: 5 g, carbs: 59g, protein: 16g, sodium: 2.5g

Kidney Bean Jambalaya

Preparation time: 20 minutes
Cooking time: 30 minutes
Servings: 10

Ingredients
- 3 tablespoons olive oil
- 1 lb. boneless, skinless chicken, cut into bite-sized pieces
- 4 tablespoons Cajun seasoning
- ½ and ¼ teaspoon kosher salt
- 1 pound sausage, sliced into ½ inch pieces
- 1 large yellow onion, diced
- 4 cloves garlic, minced
- 1 red bell pepper, cored and chopped into ½-inch pieces
- 1 green bell pepper, cored and chopped into ½-inch pieces
- 2 stalks celery, thinly sliced
- 1 tablespoon tomato paste
- 1 (15-ounce) can diced tomatoes with their juices
- 4 cups low-sodium chicken stock
- 4 cups water
- 2 cups white rice, uncooked
- ½ pound okra ends trimmed and sliced into ½-inch pieces
- 1 lb. raw peeled shrimp, tails removed
- 2 (15-ounce) cans kidney beans, drained and rinsed; or 10 ounces dry kidney beans, soaked and cooked
- 4 scallions, chopped

Direction
1. In a large stockpot/deep saucepan, heat 1 tablespoon of oil over medium heat.
2. Add the chicken pieces, 1 tablespoon Cajun seasoning, and ½ teaspoon kosher salt. Cook until the chicken is evenly browned.
3. Add the sausage slices and cook for 4-5 minutes.
4. Set the mixture aside in a container.
5. Heat the remaining oil over medium heat in the same pot/pan. Add the onion, garlic, celery, bell pepper, and 2 tablespoons of Cajun seasoning. Cook until softened and translucent, about 4-5 minutes.

6. Return the chicken mixture to the pot. Mix in the tomato paste and diced tomatoes with their juices.
7. Add the stock, water, and rice. Stir to combine.
8. Bring the mixture to a boil, then lower the heat to simmer for about 10 minutes.
9. Mix in the okra and simmer for 4-5 more minutes.
10. Season the shrimp with a pinch of salt and the remaining Cajun seasoning. Add the beans and shrimp to the pot.
11. Combine and cook for 4-5 minutes until the rice and shrimp are cooked through.
12. Serve warm and topped with scallions.

Nutrition:
Calories: 626, fat: 26g, carbs: 62g, protein: 36g, sodium: 24g

Italian Bean and Sausage Stew

Preparation time: 15 minutes
Cooking time: 1 hour and 15 minutes
Servings: 6-8

Ingredients
- 4-5 links hot or mild Italian pork sausage (casings removed)
- 2 tablespoons olive oil
- 2 stalks celery, chopped
- 3 carrots, peeled and chopped
- 1 medium onion, chopped
- 4 cloves garlic, minced
- 1 (6-ounce) can tomato paste
- 1 (28-ounce) can diced tomatoes with their juices
- 3 (15-ounce) cans beans (black beans, kidney beans, chickpeas, cannellini beans, or Romano beans), drained and rinsed; or 15 ounces dry beans (black beans, kidney beans, chickpeas, cannellini beans, or Romano beans), soaked and cooked
- 2 cups low-sodium chicken broth (or water)
- 1-2 hot red peppers, seeded and chopped, optional
- 1 tablespoon Italian seasoning
- Freshly ground black pepper and kosher salt, to taste
- ¼ cup flat-leaf parsley, chopped
- ⅓ cup fresh basil, chopped

Toppings:
Shredded cheese, Greek yogurt, chopped green onions, or more chopped flat-leaf parsley

Directions

1. In a medium/large deep saucepan, heat oil over medium heat.
2. Add the sausage and cook until evenly browned.
3. Add the celery, carrots, and onion. Cook until softened and translucent.
4. Add the garlic and cook until fragrant, about 1-2 minutes.
5. Add in the tomato paste, tomatoes, chicken broth, beans, hot red peppers, seasoning, freshly ground black pepper, kosher salt, parsley, and basil. Combine well and bring to a boil.
6. Over low heat, simmer for about 1 hour until the mixture thickens. Add more water if the stew is too thick.
7. Adjust seasonings to taste, then serve warm with your choice of toppings.

Nutrition:
Calories 498, fat: 25g, carbs: 33g, protein: 39g, sodium: 7g

Chorizo Bacon Bean Stew

Preparation time: 10 minutes
Cooking time: 40 minutes
Servings: 6-8

Ingredients

- 1½ tablespoons vegetable oil
- 7 ounces chorizo, chopped
- 3½ ounces smoked bacon, chopped
- 4 shallots, sliced
- 2 thyme sprigs
- 4 bay leaves
- 1 teaspoon smoked paprika
- 2 dried ancho chilies
- 1 (14-ounce) can black beans, drained and rinsed; or 5 ounces dry black beans, soaked and cooked
- 1 (14-ounce) can red kidney beans, drained and rinsed; or 5 ounces dry red kidney beans, soaked and cooked
- 1 teaspoon chipotle sauce
- 1 (14-ounce) can chopped tomatoes with their juices
- ½-⅓ cup water
- 1 teaspoon dry rosemary
- ½ teaspoon granulated garlic
- Salt and black pepper to taste

Directions

1. In a medium/large deep saucepan, heat oil over medium heat.
2. Add the bacon, chorizo, and shallots. Cook until the shallots soften, about 4-5 minutes.

3. Mix in the thyme sprigs, bay leaves, and smoked paprika. Add the chilies and beans, then stir to combine. Cook for 2 minutes.
4. Mix in the chipotle sauce, tomatoes, water, rosemary, and garlic. Season with salt and pepper to taste, stir to combine, and bring to a boil over high heat.
5. Reduce heat to low and let simmer for about 25-30 minutes or until the stew thickens.
6. Discard the chilies, thyme sprigs, and bay leaves. Serve warm.

Nutrition:
Calories 449, fat: 22 g, carbs: 17g, protein: 38g, sodium: 13g

Mushroom Quinoa White Bean Stew

Preparation time: 5 minutes
Cooking time: 60 minutes
Servings: 4

Ingredients
- 2 garlic cloves, minced
- 1 shallot, diced
- 1 tablespoon olive oil
- ½ pound mushrooms, diced
- 1 (15-ounce) can white beans, drained and rinsed; or 5 ounces dry white beans, soaked and cooked
- ½ cup sun-dried tomatoes, drained and diced
- 1 (28-ounce) can crushed tomatoes with their juices
- 3 tablespoons tomato paste
- 2 teaspoons Italian seasoning
- 2 cups water
- Freshly ground black pepper and kosher salt, to taste
- 2 cups cooked quinoa, to serve

Directions
1. In a medium/large Dutch oven, heat oil over medium heat.
2. Add the garlic and shallots. Cook until softened and translucent, about 1 minute.
3. Add in the mushrooms. Cook for about 2 minutes until softened.
4. Add the beans, tomatoes, beans, tomato paste, and Italian seasoning. Stir to combine.
5. Add in the water, freshly ground black pepper, and kosher salt. Bring to a boil.
6. Over low heat, simmer for about an hour.
7. Season with more freshly ground black pepper and kosher salt to taste.
8. Serve warm with cooked quinoa.

Nutrition:
Calories: 209, fat: 6g, carbs: 34g, protein: 9g, sodium: 14g

Pumpkin Bacon Bean Stew

Preparation time: 15-20 minutes
Cooking time: 2 hours
Servings: 6-8

Ingredients
- 1 lb. dried cranberry or pinto beans, soaked and cooked
- 2 tablespoons vegetable oil
- ½ pound smoked bacon, diced into small pieces
- 4 large garlic cloves, minced
- 1 large white onion, cut into ½-inch slices
- 1 green bell pepper, cored and cut into ½-inch slices
- 1 jalapeno pepper, seeded and minced
- 2 teaspoons ground cumin
- 1 teaspoon dried oregano
- 1 teaspoon sweet paprika
- Freshly ground black pepper and kosher salt, to taste
- 4 plum tomatoes, coarsely chopped
- 6 cups low-sodium chicken stock or another type of broth
- ½ pound pumpkin or butternut squash, peeled, seeded, and cut into 1-inch chunks
- 1¼ cups corn
- 2 tablespoons fresh basil, coarsely chopped

Directions
1. In a large and deep saucepan / skillet, heat oil over medium heat.
2. Add the bacon and cook until evenly crisped and browned, about 4-5 minutes.
3. Add the garlic and cook until fragrant, about 1 minute.
4. Add the bell pepper, jalapeno pepper, onion, oregano, ground cumin, 1 teaspoon freshly ground black pepper, 1 teaspoon kosher salt, and paprika. Cook until the vegetables soften, about 4-5 minutes.
5. Add the tomatoes and cook for 2 minutes or until softened.
6. Add the stock and beans, then bring to a boil.
7. Over low heat, partially cover and simmer for about 45 minutes, stirring occasionally.
8. Add the pumpkin / butternut squash and cook for about 15 minutes or until tender.
9. Mix in the corn and basil, then simmer for 10 more minutes over medium heat.
10. Season to taste with freshly ground black pepper and kosher salt.

11. Serve warm.

Nutrition:
Calories: 493, fat: 15g, carbs: 67g, protein: 9g, sodium: 4.3g

Chorizo and Bean Stew

Preparation time: 10 minutes
Cooking time: 30 minutes
Servings: 4

Ingredients
- 1 tablespoon olive oil
- 7 ounces chorizo sausage, thickly sliced
- 1 yellow onion, chopped
- 14 ounces boneless, skinless chicken breasts, cubed
- 1 medium red tomato, roughly chopped
- 1 (14-ounce) can cannellini beans, drained and rinsed; or 5 ounces dry cannellini beans, soaked and cooked
- 1 large potato, cut into small cubes
- 2 cups low-sodium chicken stock
- 4 tablespoons flat-leaf parsley, chopped

Directions
1. In a medium to large deep saucepan, heat oil over medium heat.
2. Add the onion, chorizo, and chicken. Cook for 4-5 minutes.
3. Add the tomato and cook for 2-3 minutes or until softened.
4. Add the stock, beans, and potato. Stir gently to combine, then bring to a boil.
5. Over low heat, simmer until chicken is cooked through and potatoes are tender, about 20 minutes.
6. Top with the parsley and serve warm.

Nutrition:
Calories: 433, fat: 19g, carbs: 25g, protein 43g, sodium: 3042mg

Lamb Bean Stew
Preparation time: 50-60 minutes
Cooking time: 2 hours
Servings: 8

Ingredients
- 2 lbs. lamb stew meat, cut into bite-sized pieces
- 2 cups white onion, finely diced
- 1 ½ cups celery, finely diced

- 2½ cups carrots, peeled and finely diced
- 4 cloves garlic, minced
- 1 tablespoon fresh rosemary, minced
- 1 tablespoon fresh thyme, leaves only, minced
- 1 lb. Great Northern beans, soaked and cooked
- 4 cups low-sodium chicken stock
- 1½ teaspoons kosher salt
- 1½ teaspoons freshly ground black pepper
- ½ cup all-purpose flour
- ½ teaspoon ground coriander

Directions
1. In a large mixing bowl, add the flour, ½ teaspoon freshly ground black pepper, ½ teaspoon kosher salt, and ground coriander. Combine well.
2. Add the lamb pieces and toss to coat well.
3. In a medium to large stockpot/Dutch oven, heat oil over medium heat.
4. Add the lamb pieces and cook until evenly browned.
5. Add the onion, garlic, and celery. Cook until softened and translucent, about 3-5 minutes.
6. Add the rosemary, thyme, stock, beans, 1 teaspoon kosher salt, and 1 teaspoon freshly ground black pepper. Bring to a boil.
7. Over low heat, add the carrots and simmer until meat is cooked through, about 2 hours while stirring occasionally.
8. Season to taste with more freshly ground black pepper and kosher salt.
9. Serve warm.

Nutrition:
Calories: 377, fat: 9g, carbs: 25g, protein: 44g, sodium: 1038mg

Apricot Chickpea Stew

Preparation time: 10 minutes
Cooking time: 30 minutes
Servings: 4

Ingredients
- ¼ cup low-sodium vegetable broth
- 1 small sweet white onion, chopped
- 1 bell pepper, cored and diced
- 1 leek, rinsed, and sliced into ¼-inch rounds
- 3-4 medium carrots, peeled and sliced
- 1 (15-ounce) can garbanzo beans, drained and rinsed; or 5 ounces dry garbanzo beans, soaked and cooked
- ¼ teaspoon garlic powder
- 2 teaspoons curry powder
- 2 teaspoons ground cumin

- 1½ teaspoons sweet paprika
- ½ teaspoon ground turmeric
- ⅛ teaspoon ground ginger
- Pinch of ground cinnamon
- 2½ cups low-sodium vegetable broth
- ½ cup packed dried apricots, roughly chopped or whole
- ¼ cup black olives, pitted and sliced
- A handful of cilantro, roughly chopped
- Cooked quinoa or cooked grain of your choice

Directions
1. In a medium to large stockpot/deep saucepan/Dutch oven, add a splash of broth and heat it over medium heat.
2. Add the onion, leek, and bell pepper. Cook until the veggies have softened and turned translucent, about 4-5 minutes.
3. Add the carrots, beans, garlic powder, and all the spices. Combine well and cook for 1 minute.
4. Add the black olives, broth, and dried apricots. Stir gently, then bring to a boil.
5. Over low heat, cover and simmer for about 20 minutes or until the vegetables are tender.
6. Top with a handful of cilantro. Serve warm with cooked quinoa or your choice of cooked grain.

Nutrition:
Calories: 324, fat: 9g, carbs: 43g, protein: 20g, sodium: 791mg

Black Bean Veggie Stew

Preparation time: 5-10 minutes
Cooking time: 50 minutes
Servings: 5

Ingredients
- 1 tablespoon olive oil
- ½ cup red bell pepper, cored and chopped
- 2 large onions, chopped
- ½ cup celery, chopped
- ½ cup carrot, peeled and chopped
- ¼ cup dry sherry or low-sodium chicken broth
- 2 tablespoons garlic, minced
- 1 (14.5-ounce) can diced tomatoes with their juices
- 2 tablespoons tomato paste
- 3 (15-ounce) cans black beans, drained and rinsed; or 15 ounces dry black beans, soaked and cooked
- 1 (14.5-ounce) container low-sodium chicken broth

- 2 tablespoons honey
- 2 teaspoons ground cumin
- 4 teaspoons chili powder
- ½ teaspoon dried oregano
- ¼ cup cilantro, minced
- 5 tablespoons Monterey Jack cheese, shredded
- 5 tablespoons low-fat sour cream
- 2 tablespoons green onion, chopped

Directions
1. In a medium to large Dutch oven, heat oil and sherry over medium heat.
2. Add the onions, red bell pepper, carrot, and celery. Cook until softened and translucent.
3. Add the garlic and cook until fragrant, about 1 minute.
4. Add the tomatoes, tomato paste, beans, broth, honey, ground cumin, chili powder, and oregano. Bring to a boil.
5. Over low heat, cover, and let simmer for about 40 minutes.
6. Add the cilantro and simmer until the stew has thickened, about 10-15 minutes.
7. Garnish with sour cream, Monterey Jack cheese, and chopped green onion.
8. Serve warm.

Nutrition:
Calories: 385, fat: 7g, carbs: 61g, protein 19g, sodium 922mg

Turkey Three Bean Chili

Preparation time: 10 minutes
Cooking time: 4 hours and 10 minutes
Servings: 10

Ingredients
- 1 (20-ounce) package ground turkey, 93% lean
- 1 (4.5-ounce) can chopped green chiles
- 1 (28-ounce) can fire-roasted diced tomatoes with their juices
- 1 (16-ounce) can tomato sauce
- 1 small onion, chopped
- 2 tablespoons chili powder
- 1 (15-ounce) can pinto beans, drained and rinsed; or 5 ounces dry pinto beans, soaked and cooked
- 1 (15-ounce) can kidney beans, drained and rinsed; or 5 ounces dry kidney beans, soaked and cooked
- 1 (15-ounce) can black beans, drained and rinsed; or 5 ounces dry black beans, soaked and cooked

- 1 tablespoon garlic, minced
- 1 teaspoon dried oregano
- 1 pinch ground cumin

Directions

1. Spray a large deep saucepan or skillet with cooking spray and heat over medium heat.
2. Add the turkey and cook until evenly browned, about 8-10 minutes.
3. In a slow cooker, add the ground turkey, green chilies, diced tomatoes, tomato sauce, onion, chili powder, garlic, all the beans, oregano, and ground cumin. Stir until well-combined.
4. Close the lid and ensure it's in the sealing position. Select the HIGH setting and set the timer for 4 hours (if cooking using the LOW mode, set a timer for 7 hours).
5. When the time is up, serve.

Nutrition:

Calories: 238, fat: 5g, carbs: 29g, protein 20g, sodium: 877 mg

Classic Black Bean Chili

Preparation time: 5 minutes
Cooking time: 35-40 minutes
Servings: 4

Ingredients

- ¼ cup olive oil
- 2 medium red bell peppers, cored and coarsely chopped
- 2 cups yellow onion, chopped
- 6 garlic cloves, chopped
- 2 teaspoons dried oregano
- 2 tablespoons chili powder
- 1½ teaspoons ground cumin
- ½ teaspoon cayenne pepper
- 3 (15-ounce) cans black beans, drained (but reserve ½ cup of the bean liquid); or 5 ounces dry black beans, soaked and cooked
- 1 (16-ounce) can tomato sauce

For the garnish:
Sour cream, grated Monterey Jack cheese, chopped cilantro, and chopped green onion.

Directions

1. In a medium to large stockpot/deep saucepan/Dutch oven, heat oil over medium heat.
2. Add in the bell peppers, garlic, and onion. Cook until softened and translucent, about 8-10 minutes.
3. Add the oregano, chili powder, ground cumin, and cayenne pepper. Cook for 2 minutes.
4. Add in the tomato sauce, beans, and reserved bean liquid. Bring to a boil.
5. Over medium-low heat, simmer the mixture for about 15 minutes.
6. Season to taste with freshly ground black pepper and kosher salt.
7. Divide the chili into serving bowls. Top with sour cream, grated cheese, chopped cilantro, and chopped green onion.
8. Serve warm.

Nutrition:
Calories: 434, fat: 15g, carbs: 43g, protein: 12g, sodium: 736mg

Apple Beans with Rice and Chicken

Preparation time: 15 minutes
Cooking time: 20 minutes
Servings: 4-6

Ingredients

- 1 cup Granny Smith apples, peeled and chopped
- ½ cup cilantro, chopped
- ⅓ cup red onion, finely chopped
- 1 teaspoon lime juice or to taste
- ⅓ cup green bell pepper, cored and finely chopped
- 2 tablespoons vegetable oil
- 1 teaspoon ground coriander
- 1½ teaspoons chili powder
- ¾ teaspoon cumin seeds
- 3 garlic cloves, minced
- 3 cups low-sodium chicken broth
- 2 (15-ounce) cans black beans, drained and rinsed; or 10 ounces dry black beans, soaked and cooked
- Freshly ground black pepper and kosher salt, to taste
- 4 cups brown or white rice, cooked
- 1 (2 to 3 pound) rotisserie chicken, skin removed and shredded
- 4-6 lime wedges

Directions

1. In a large mixing bowl, add ¼ cup cilantro, the apple, 2 tablespoons onion, and ½ teaspoon lime juice. Combine until mixed well.
2. In a medium saucepan or skillet, heat oil over medium heat.
3. Add the bell pepper and remaining onion. Cook for 6-7 minutes until softened and translucent.
4. Add the ground coriander, chili powder, ground cumin, and garlic. Cook for 2 minutes.
5. Mix in the beans and broth, then bring to a boil.
6. Over medium-low heat, simmer for about 8-10 minutes until sauce is thickened.
7. Season to taste with freshly ground black pepper, kosher salt, and more lime juice.
8. Divide the bean mixture between serving plates. Top with the chicken and apple salsa.
9. Serve with the remaining cilantro on top and lime wedges.

Nutrition:
Calories: 674, fat: 32g, carbs: 44g, protein: 38g, sodium: 1147mg

BBQ Pork Beans

Preparation time: 15 minutes
Cooking time: 10 minutes
Servings: 4

Ingredients
- 2 tablespoons brown sugar, packed
- 1 cup barbecue sauce
- 2 tablespoons white vinegar
- 1 (15-ounce) can navy beans, drained and rinsed; or 5 ounces dry navy beans, soaked and cooked
- 2 tablespoons canola or vegetable oil
- ½ teaspoon kosher salt
- ¼ teaspoon freshly ground black pepper
- 4 boneless center-cut pork chops, about ½-inch thick

Directions
1. In a large mixing bowl, add the brown sugar, barbecue sauce, vinegar, and beans. Combine until well-mixed.
2. Season the pork chops with freshly ground black pepper and kosher salt.
3. In a medium saucepan or skillet, heat oil over medium-high heat.
4. Add the pork chops and cook until they are evenly browned, flipping once, for about 5-6 minutes.
5. Over medium heat, add the bean mixture and cook until the pork is no longer pinkish about 3-5 minutes.
6. Serve warm.

Nutrition:
Calories: 650; fat: 26g, carbs: 61g, protein: 42g, sodium: 1430mg

Baked Eggs Bean Meal

Preparation time: 5 minutes
Cooking time: 25 minutes
Servings: 4-6

Ingredients
- 2 tablespoons olive oil
- ½ pound sweet or spicy Italian sausage, casings removed, optional
- 1 medium yellow onion, thinly sliced
- 1 (15-ounce) can chickpeas or white beans, drained and rinsed; or 5 ounces dry chickpeas/white beans, soaked and cooked
- 2 garlic cloves, finely chopped
- Kosher salt, to taste
- 1 (28-ounce) can whole tomatoes, somewhat crushed
- 4 cups leafy greens such as kale, spinach, or Swiss chard, stemmed and roughly chopped
- 6 large eggs
- Freshly ground black pepper, to taste
- 2 tablespoons mixed fresh herbs of your choice, chopped (Italian parsley, basil, etc.)
- Pecorino or parmesan cheese, grated, optional

Directions
1. Preheat the oven to 375°F (190°C).
2. In a 12-inch oven-proof skillet, heat oil over medium heat.
3. If using, add the sausage, breaking it into small pieces using a spatula. Cook until cooked through and crisp, about 7-8 minutes. Set aside on a plate lined with a paper towel.
4. Add the onion and cook for about 3-5 minutes or until softened and translucent.
5. Season with kosher salt to taste, then add the cooked sausage and tomatoes.
6. Add the greens and simmer until the greens have wilted. Season to taste with more kosher salt.
7. Create six pockets in the mixture and crack the eggs in them.
8. Season the eggs with more freshly ground black pepper and kosher salt.
9. Add the skillet to the oven, then bake for 7-9 minutes or until eggs are well-set.
10. Serve with fresh herbs and grated cheese on top, if desired.

Nutrition:
Calories: 366, fat: 23g, carbs: 19g, protein: 20g, sodium: 1345mg

Iranian Lima Beans, Dill, and Eggs

Preparation time: 5 minutes
Cooking time: 10 minutes
Servings: 2

Ingredients
- 3 tablespoon unsalted butter
- 1 large onion, sliced
- ½ teaspoon ground turmeric
- 4 cloves garlic, chopped
- 2 (14-ounce) cans white beans or lima beans, drained and rinsed; or 10 ounces dry white beans, soaked and cooked
- Juice of ¼ lemon
- ½ teaspoon ground cumin
- 1 teaspoon sugar or honey
- Kosher salt, to taste
- 1 teaspoon lemon zest
- ½ cup mini tomatoes
- ½ bunch fresh dill, chopped
- Freshly ground black pepper and kosher salt, to taste
- 4 large eggs
- Sliced bread, to serve

Directions
1. In a medium saucepan or skillet, heat the butter over medium heat.
2. Add the onion and cook for about 3 minutes or until softened and translucent.
3. Add the ground turmeric and garlic, then cook until fragrant and light golden, about 1 minute.
4. Add the beans, lemon juice, ground cumin, and 1 cup of water. Add the sugar/honey and ½ teaspoon of kosher salt.
5. Bring to a boil. Add the tomatoes, dill, and lemon zest. Season with more freshly ground black pepper and kosher salt.
6. Reduce to low heat, then create four pockets and crack the eggs in them.
7. Cover and simmer the mixture for about 4 minutes or until the yolks are runny and the whites are set.
8. Serve warm with sliced bread.

Nutrition:
Calories: 658, fat: 32g, carbs: 77g, protein: 35g, sodium: 1395mg

Zucchini Pinto Bean Enchiladas

Preparation time: 20 minutes
Cooking time: 30 minutes
Servings: 6

Ingredients
- 1 (14.5-ounce) can diced tomatoes, drained
- 1 medium zucchini, diced
- 1 (12-ounce) bag frozen corn, thawed
- 1 (15-ounce) can pinto beans, drained and rinsed; or 5 ounces dry pinto beans, soaked and cooked
- 1 (4.5-ounce) can chopped green chilies
- 2 cups cheddar cheese, shredded
- 1 cup Monterey Jack cheese, shredded
- Freshly ground black pepper and kosher salt, to taste
- 12 (8-inch) flour tortillas
- 1 cup enchilada sauce

Directions
1. Preheat the oven to 400°F (200°C). Grease a 13" by 9" baking dish with cooking spray or cooking oil, then line with foil or parchment paper.
2. In a large mixing bowl, add the tomatoes, zucchini, corn, beans, chilies, ½ cup Monterey Jack cheese, and 1 cup cheddar cheese. Season with freshly ground black pepper and kosher salt. Combine until well-mixed.
3. Using damp paper towels, arrange the tortillas and wrap them up in the towels.
4. Microwave for 30 seconds on the HIGH setting.
5. Spoon the bean filling over the tortillas and roll them up tightly.
6. Seam-side down, arrange the tortillas into the baking dish.
7. Pour the enchilada sauce over the tortillas and sprinkle the remaining cheese on top.
8. Bake for about 30 minutes or until the cheese is bubbly.
9. Serve warm.

Nutrition:
Calories: 678, fat: 26g, carbs: 87g, protein: 29g, sodium: 1723mg

Chapter 3: Dinner

Lamb and Beans with Sun-Dried Tomatoes

Preparation time: 30 minutes
Cooking time: 20 minutes
Servings: 4

Ingredients
- 2 tablespoons olive oil
- 4 (6-ounce each) loin lamb chops, about 1¼ inches thick
- Kosher salt and freshly ground black pepper, to taste
- 1 medium onion, finely chopped
- 4 cloves garlic, sliced
- ¼ to ½ teaspoon crushed red pepper flakes
- 1 tablespoon chopped fresh rosemary or 1 teaspoon dried rosemary, optional
- ½ cup sun-dried tomatoes, drained and slivered
- 2 (15-ounce) cans cannellini beans, drained and rinsed; or 10 ounces dry cannellini beans, soaked and cooked
- ½ cup water

Directions
1. Season the lamb chops generously with freshly ground black pepper and kosher salt.
2. In a medium saucepan or skillet, heat oil over medium-high heat.
3. Add the lamb chops and cook until evenly browned, about 3-4 minutes. Set aside and leave the lamb fat and oil in the pan.
4. Using the same saucepan or skillet, add the onion, garlic, freshly ground black pepper, kosher salt, crushed red pepper flakes, and rosemary. Cook until the onion has softened, about 3-5 minutes.
5. Add the tomatoes, beans, and ½ cup water. Bring to a boil.
6. Over medium-low heat, simmer for about 5 minutes until thickened.
7. Add the lamb chops back to the pan, then cover and simmer for another 3-4 minutes.
8. Serve warm with some rosemary on top.

Nutrition:
Calories: 603, fat: 27g, carbs: 53g, protein: 37g, sodium: 486 mg

Southern Pork and Cannellini Beans

Preparation time: 10 minutes
Cooking time: 30 minutes
Servings: 4

Ingredients

- 1 yellow onion, sliced
- 5½ ounces gammon steak, fat trimmed and cut into bite-sized pieces
- 9 ounces pork tenderloin filet, fat trimmed and cut into bite-sized pieces
- 2 garlic cloves, crushed
- 2 teaspoons smoked paprika
- ½ teaspoon hot chili powder
- 2 (14-ounce) cans cannellini beans, drained and rinsed; or 10 ounces dry cannellini beans, soaked and cooked
- 1 (14-ounce) can chopped tomatoes with their juices
- 2 tablespoons tomato purée
- 2 teaspoons prepared English mustard
- 1¾ cups low-sodium pork or chicken stock
- 3 heaping tablespoons flat-leaf parsley, chopped
- 4 tablespoons low-fat plain yogurt
- Freshly ground black pepper and kosher salt, to taste

Directions

1. Spray a medium saucepan or skillet with cooking oil and heat up over medium heat.
2. Add the onion and cook until softened and translucent, about 4-5 minutes.
3. Season the gammon and pork with freshly ground black pepper. Add to the skillet and cook for 2 minutes.
4. Add the garlic, chili powder, and paprika, then cook for a few seconds.
5. Add the beans, tomato puree, mustard, and tomatoes. Add the stock and then stir gently. Bring to a simmer.
6. Cook until the pork is cooked through, and the mixture has thickened, about 20-25 minutes.
7. Add half the chopped parsley and stir.
8. Serve warm with the remaining parsley on top along with a dollop of yogurt.

Nutrition:
Calories: 322, fat: 8g, carbs: 36g, protein: 32g, sodium: 364 mg

Bean Corn Chicken Skillet

Preparation time: 15 minutes
Cooking time: 15 minutes
Servings: 6

Ingredients

- 3 tablespoons olive oil
- 1 medium red onion, diced
- 1½ pounds boneless, skinless chicken breasts, cut into bite-sized pieces

- 1 large red bell pepper, cored and diced
- 1 (4-ounce) can diced green chilies (do not drain)
- 1 (8-ounce) can corn, drained and rinsed
- 1 (15-ounce) can black beans, drained and rinsed; or 5 ounces dry black beans, soaked and cooked
- 1 teaspoon kosher salt, or to taste
- ½ teaspoon freshly ground black pepper, or to taste
- 1-2 teaspoons ground cumin
- 1-2 teaspoons chili powder
- ½ teaspoon ground coriander
- 2-4 tablespoons lime juice
- 2-3 tablespoons cilantro, chopped

Directions
1. In a large saucepan or skillet, heat oil over medium heat.
2. Add the onion and cook until softened and translucent, about 4-5 minutes.
3. Add the chicken and bell pepper. Cook for about 5-7 minutes.
4. Add the green chiles, corn, beans, kosher salt, freshly ground black pepper, ground cumin, chili powder, and ground coriander. Stir and simmer until mixture is warmed through, about 2-3 minutes.
5. Add the lemon juice and adjust the seasonings to taste.
6. Top with the cilantro and serve warm.

Nutrition:
Calories: 393, fat: 12g, carbs: 29g, protein: 43g, sodium: 781mg

Sausage Bean Skillet

Preparation time: 10 minutes
Cooking time: 20 minutes
Servings: 4

Ingredients
- 2 tablespoons olive oil
- 12-14 ounces Italian or smoked sausage links (pork or chicken), cooked and sliced into ¼-inch pieces
- 3 garlic cloves, minced
- 2 (15-ounce) cans white beans (butter beans, Great Northern, or cannellini), drained and rinsed; or 10 ounces dry white beans (butter beans, Great Northern, or cannellini), soaked and cooked
- 1½ cups low-sodium chicken stock
- 1 teaspoon fresh thyme leaves, minced
- ½ teaspoon kosher salt
- ¼ teaspoon freshly ground black pepper

- ½ bunch (packed 3 cups) curly kale, stemmed and torn into bite-sized pieces
- 1 tablespoon lemon juice
- ½ cup parmesan cheese, grated
- Crushed red pepper flakes, optional

Directions
1. In a medium-large saucepan or skillet, heat oil over medium heat.
2. Add the sausage and cook until evenly browned about 4-5 minutes. Set aside to drain on a plate lined with a paper towel.
3. Add the garlic and cook until fragrant, about 15 seconds.
4. Add the beans (⅔ of the entire portion), 1 cup stock, thyme, freshly ground black pepper and kosher salt. Stir well and bring to a simmer.
5. In a medium mixing bowl, add the remaining beans. Mash them to get a paste-like consistency.
6. Add the mashed beans to the skillet, then simmer for 2-3 minutes or until the mixture is warmed through.
7. Add the kale and simmer over medium-low heat until wilted, about 2-3 minutes.
8. Add the sausage, lemon juice, and parmesan cheese. Add the remaining stock and stir to combine.
9. Top with crushed red pepper flakes and parmesan cheese, if desired.
10. Serve warm with some crusty bread.

Nutrition:
Calories: 547, fat: 37g, carbs: 25g, protein: 31g, sodium: 1498mg

Brown Rice Bean Skillet

Preparation time: 5 minutes
Cooking time: 10 minutes
Servings: 4

Ingredients
- 1 tablespoon avocado or olive oil
- ¼ cup red onion, diced
- ½ teaspoon smoked paprika
- ½ teaspoon dried oregano
- 2 cups brown rice, cooked
- 1 (10-ounce) can diced tomatoes with green chilies, drained
- 1 (15-ounce) can black beans, drained and rinsed; or 5 ounces dry black beans, soaked and cooked
- ½ cup Monterey Jack cheese, shredded

For the garnish:
Chopped cilantro, chopped green onions, sliced avocado, sliced jalapeno peppers

Directions

1. In a medium oven-safe saucepan or skillet, heat oil over medium heat.
2. Add the onion and paprika. Cook until softened and translucent, about 3 minutes.
3. Add the tomatoes, rice, and beans. Cook for 3-5 minutes or until heated through.
4. Sprinkle cheese over the mixture.
5. Preheat the oven to the BROIL setting.
6. Broil until the cheese turns golden-brown, about 2-3 minutes.
7. Garnish with the toppings of your choice and serve.

Nutrition:
Calories: 283, fat: 9g, carbs: 40g, protein: 12g, sodium: 78mg

Navy Bean Potato Skillet

Preparation time: 15-20 minutes
Cooking time: 25-30 minutes
Servings: 4

Ingredients

- 4½ tablespoons olive oil
- 1 yellow onion, thinly sliced
- 1 large yellow potato, scrubbed and diced
- ¾ teaspoons kosher salt
- ¾ teaspoons smoked paprika or sweet paprika
- 4 cups cabbage, thinly sliced
- 1 tablespoon white wine vinegar
- 1 (15-ounce) can navy beans, drained and rinsed; or 5 ounces dry navy beans, soaked and cooked
- 4 large eggs
- ½ cup plain yogurt of your choice
- ¼ cup fresh dill, chopped
- Lemon wedges, to serve

Directions

1. In a medium saucepan or skillet, heat 4 tablespoons of oil over medium heat.
2. Add the potatoes, onion, paprika, and a pinch of kosher salt. Cook until the potatoes have softened and are beginning to brown, about 6-7 minutes.
3. Add ⅓ cup water as well as the vinegar, and cabbage. Stir gently and cover.
4. Simmer for 4-5 minutes or until the cabbage has softened.

5. Uncover and simmer for 4-5 more minutes until the mixture thickens and the cabbage turns brown.
6. Add the beans and cook for 3-4 minutes.
7. In another medium saucepan or skillet, heat the remaining oil over medium heat.
8. Add the eggs and remaining kosher salt, then cook for 2-3 minutes or until the egg whites are runny.
9. In a small bowl, combine the dill and yogurt, reserving some of the dill.
10. Divide the bean mixture into serving plates and top with the yogurt sauce, fried eggs, and reserved dill.
11. Serve warm with some lemon wedges.

Nutrition:
Calories: 432, fat: 23g, carbs: 41g, protein: 18g, sodium: 939mg

Mushroom Bean Broccoli Skillet

Preparation time: 15 minutes
Cooking time: 18 minutes
Servings: 6

Ingredients
- 8-12 ounces broccoli, cut into florets; or broccolini or broccoli rabe, trimmed and cut into small pieces
- 2 tablespoons extra-virgin olive oil
- 1 small onion, finely chopped; or 2-3 shallots, finely chopped
- 3-4 cloves garlic, minced
- ¼ cup water or dry white wine
- ⅔ cup cured black olives, pitted and halved
- 1 (15-ounce) can cannellini beans or white beans
- 1 (14.5-ounce) can diced tomatoes with their juices
- 8 ounces cremini mushrooms, stemmed and sliced
- ¼ cup flat-leaf parsley, minced
- Freshly ground black pepper and kosher salt, to taste
- Fresh basil, sliced, optional

Directions
1. In a medium saucepan or skillet, heat oil over medium heat.
2. Add the onions/shallots and garlic. Cook until softened and golden, about 2 minutes.
3. Add the water/wine and broccoli florets/broccolini. Cover and cook for 2 minutes or until bright green.
4. Add in the olives, beans, tomatoes, and mushrooms. Stir and simmer for 7-8 minutes or until broccoli becomes tender.
5. Add the parsley, freshly ground black pepper, and salt to taste, then stir well.

6. Top with the basil, if desired, and serve warm.

Nutrition:
Calories: 224, fat: 8g, carbs: 17g, protein: 12g, sodium: 184mg

Tuscan Artichoke Bean Skillet

Preparation time: 5 minutes
Cooking time: 25 minutes
Servings: 4

Ingredients
- 2 tablespoons extra-virgin olive oil
- 8 ounces brown mushrooms, sliced
- 1 ½ cups yellow onion (about 1 large onion), diced
- 3 cloves garlic, minced
- ⅔ cup oil-packed sun-dried tomatoes, drained and chopped
- 1 (14.5-ounce) can artichoke hearts, rinsed and quartered
- 2 (14.5-ounce) cans fire-roasted diced tomatoes with their juices
- 2 (14.5-ounce) cans cannellini beans, drained and rinsed; or 10 ounces dry cannellini beans, soaked and cooked
- ½ teaspoon kosher salt
- ½ teaspoon freshly ground black pepper
- 1 teaspoon dried oregano
- ½ teaspoon dried thyme
- 1 teaspoon granulated sugar
- Chopped flat-leaf parsley, for garnish
- Crusty bread, to serve

Directions
1. In a medium saucepan or skillet, heat 1 tablespoon of oil over medium heat.
2. Add the mushrooms and cook until softened and evenly browned, about 3-4 minutes. Then set aside.
3. Add the remaining oil and onion. Cook until softened and lightly browned, about 2-3 minutes.
4. Add the garlic and sun-dried tomatoes. Cook until fragrant and softened for about 2 minutes.
5. Add the artichoke hearts, diced tomatoes with their juices, beans, thyme, oregano, freshly ground black pepper, kosher salt, and sugar.
6. Over medium-low heat, cover, and simmer for about 10 minutes or until warmed through.
7. Add the mushrooms back to the pan and stir gently.
8. Top with the parsley and serve warm with some crusty bread.

Nutrition:
Calories: 264, fat: 12g, carbs: 38g, protein: 9g, sodium: 539mg

Thai Chicken Broccoli Bean Wrap

Preparation time: 10 minutes
Cooking time 15 minutes
Servings: 4

Ingredients
- 1 tablespoon vegetable oil
- ½ pound boneless, skinless chicken breasts, cut into ½-inch cubes
- 1 tablespoon fresh ginger or ginger root, finely chopped
- 2 small garlic cloves, finely chopped
- 2 cups small broccoli florets
- 1 small onion, chopped
- ½ medium green bell pepper, cored and chopped
- 1 (15.5-ounce) can white beans, drained and rinsed; or 5 ounces dry white beans, soaked and cooked
- 2 tablespoons low-sodium tamari soy sauce
- 2 tablespoons lemon zest
- 2 tablespoons cilantro, finely chopped
- 1 tablespoon brown sugar
- 1 tablespoon low-fat peanut butter
- ¼ teaspoon crushed red pepper flakes
- 6 (10-inch) flour tortillas, warmed
- Thai dipping sauce or dipping sauce of your choice

Direction
1. In a medium wok or deep saucepan, heat oil over medium-high heat.
2. Add the chicken and cook until evenly browned on each side, about 3-4 minutes.
3. Add the broccoli, ginger root, garlic, onion, and bell pepper. Cook until vegetables are tender, about 4-5 minutes.
4. Add the beans and other ingredients. Cook for 2-3 minutes or until warmed through.
5. To make the wraps, add ¾ cup bean mixture in the center of each tortilla, then roll over to seal the wraps.
6. Serve with Thai dipping sauce or dipping sauce of your choice.

Nutrition:
Calories: 280, fat: 7g, carbs: 41g, protein: 18g, sodium: 620mg

White Bean Chili Wraps

Preparation time: 10 minutes
Cooking time: 0 minutes
Servings: 4

Ingredients
2 teaspoons canned and finely chopped chipotles in adobo sauce
2 tablespoons apple cider vinegar
1 tablespoon canola oil
¼ teaspoon kosher salt
¼ cup cilantro, chopped
2 cups red cabbage, shredded
1 medium carrot, peeled and shredded
1 (15-ounce) can white beans, drained and rinsed; or 5 ounces dry white beans, soaked and cooked
1 ripe avocado, pitted and chopped
½ cup sharp cheddar cheese, shredded
2 tablespoons red onion, minced
4 (8-10 inch) tortillas or whole-wheat wraps

Directions
1. In a large mixing bowl, add the chipotle, vinegar, oil, and kosher salt. Mix until well-combined.
2. Add the cilantro, cabbage, and carrot. Toss to mix well.
3. In another bowl, add the avocado and beans. Mash until smooth, then add the onion and cheese. Mix until well-combined.
4. To make the wraps, add ½ cup of the bean mixture in the center of each tortilla.
5. Add ⅔ cup cabbage slaw to each tortilla, then roll the tortillas to seal the wraps.
6. Serve fresh.

Nutrition:
Calories 346, fat: 17g, carbs: 44g, protein: 12g, sodium: 465mg

Chicken Spinach Bean Wrap

Preparation time: 10-15 minutes
Cooking time: 0 minutes
Servings: 4

Ingredients
- 2 teaspoon lemon juice
- 1 small garlic clove, minced

- 1 (15-ounce) white beans (navy or cannellini), drained and rinsed; or 5 ounces dry white beans (navy or cannellini), soaked and cooked
- 3 tablespoons extra-virgin olive oil
- 1 teaspoon thyme leaves
- Pinch of kosher salt
- ¼ teaspoon freshly ground black pepper
- 4 large (10-12-inch) flour tortillas
- ¾ pound roasted deli chicken breast, thinly sliced
- 1 large tomato, thinly sliced
- ¼ medium red onion, thinly sliced
- 2 ounces parmesan cheese, shaved
- 1 cup baby spinach leaves

Directions

1. In a food processor or blender, add the lemon juice, garlic, beans, oil, thyme, freshly ground black pepper, and kosher salt.
2. Blend until smooth.
3. To make the wraps, add ⅔ of the bean mixture in the center of each tortilla.
4. Place the sliced chicken over the bean mixture, followed by a layer of tomato, onion, cheese, and spinach. Roll the tortillas up to seal the wraps.
5. Serve fresh.

Nutrition:
Calories: 447, fat: 17g, carbs: 45g, protein: 29g, sodium: 145mg

Bean Avocado Tacos

Preparation time: 15 minutes
Cooking time: 10 minutes
Servings: 4

Ingredients
For the bean mixture:
- 1 tablespoon olive oil
- ½ small yellow onion, diced
- 1 garlic clove, minced
- ½ teaspoon ground cumin
- ¼ teaspoon smoked paprika
- ⅛ teaspoon cayenne pepper
- ½ teaspoon kosher salt
- Freshly ground black pepper, to taste
- 1 (15-ounce) can black beans, drained and rinsed; or 5 ounces dry black beans, soaked and cooked
- 1 tablespoon tomato paste

- 1 tablespoon water

For the tacos:
- 8 hard or soft corn taco shells
- 1 avocado, pitted and peeled
- Juice from ½ lime
- Pinch of kosher salt and freshly ground black pepper
- ½ cup cheddar cheese, shredded
- 1 plum tomato, diced
- 1 cup romaine lettuce, shredded

Directions
1. Bake the tacos per the package directions in a preheated oven for about 6-7 minutes.
2. In a medium saucepan or skillet, heat oil over medium heat.
3. Add the onion and cook until softened and translucent, about 2-3 minutes.
4. Add the garlic and cook until fragrant, about 30 seconds.
5. Add the ground cumin, paprika, cayenne pepper, freshly ground black pepper, kosher salt, beans, tomato paste, and water. Cook until heated through, about 2-3 minutes.
6. In a medium mixing bowl, add the avocado and mash using a fork. Season with freshly ground black pepper and kosher salt, then add the lime juice. Mix until well-combined.
7. To assemble the tacos, add the bean mixture and the avocado mixture evenly in the center of each taco. Divide the cheese, tomatoes, and lettuce over each tortilla.
8. Serve fresh.

Nutrition:
Calories: 367, fat: 15.5g, carbs: 42g, protein: 13g, sodium: 669mg

Coconut Bean Rice

Preparation time: 5 minutes
Cooking time 25 minutes
Servings: 6-8

Ingredients
- 2 tablespoons vegetable oil
- ½ medium yellow onion, chopped
- 4 garlic cloves, chopped
- 2 cups long-grain rice
- 2 cups full-fat unsweetened coconut milk
- 1 cup water
- 1 cup low-sodium chicken stock or vegetable stock

- 1 teaspoon kosher salt
- 1 teaspoon fresh ginger, grated
- 1 (15-ounce) can kidney beans, drained and rinsed; or 5 ounces dry kidney beans, soaked and cooked
- 2 teaspoons dried thyme
- 1 Scotch bonnet or whole habanero chili
- Lime wedges, to serve, optional

Directions

1. In a medium saucepan or skillet, heat oil over medium heat.
2. Add the onion and cook until softened and translucent, about 4-5 minutes.
3. Add the garlic and rice. Cook for another 2-3 minutes.
4. Add the coconut milk, water, stock, ginger, and kosher salt.
5. Add the beans and thyme. Add the Scotch bonnet or whole habanero chili and stir gently.
6. Bring to a boil.
7. Over low heat, cover and simmer until the rice is cooked through, about 15-20 minutes.
8. Remove from the heat and use a fork to fluff the rice.
9. Remove the chili and serve garnished with some lime wedges.

Nutrition:
Calories: 217, fat: 7g, carbs: 32g, protein: 11g, sodium: 574mg

Rice, Bean, and Sausage Meal

Preparation time: 15-20 minutes
Cooking time: 40 minutes
Servings: 6-8

Ingredients
1 cup basmati rice
1 tablespoon vegetable oil
1 (12.8-ounce) package smoked Andouille sausage, thinly sliced
1 medium sweet onion, diced
1 green bell pepper, cored and diced
2 stalks celery, diced
3 cloves garlic, minced
2 tablespoons tomato paste
1½ teaspoons no-salt-added Cajun seasoning
1 teaspoon hot sauce
3 cups low-sodium chicken stock
1 bay leaf
3 (15-ounce) cans red beans, drained and rinsed; or 15 ounces dry red beans, soaked and cooked
Kosher salt and freshly ground black pepper, to taste

2 tablespoons flat-leaf parsley, chopped

Directions
1. In a large saucepan, cook the rice with 2 cups of water over medium-high heat following the package's instructions.
2. Once the rice is cooked through, drain, and set aside.
3. In a large stockpot/Dutch oven, heat oil over medium heat.
4. Add the sausage and cook for 3-4 minutes or until evenly browned. Set aside to drain on a plate lined with a paper towel.
5. Add the bell pepper, onion, and celery. Cook until tender, about 3-4 minutes.
6. Add the garlic, tomato paste, and Cajun seasoning. Cook for 1 minute or until fragrant.
7. Add the hot sauce, stock, bay leaf, beans, and sausage. Season with freshly ground black pepper and salt to taste.
8. Bring to a boil.
9. Over low heat, cover, and simmer for about 15 minutes.
10. Remove the cover and simmer until the mixture thickens, about another 15 minutes.
11. Mash the beans slightly if you want to and then season with freshly ground black pepper and kosher salt to taste. Top with the parsley.
12. Serve warm with the cooked rice.

Nutrition:
Calories: 355, fat: 12 g, carbs: 37g, protein: 15g, sodium: 884mg

Turkey Bean One-Pot Rice

Servings: 6-8
Preparation time: 10 minutes
Cooking time: 55 minutes

Ingredients
1 tablespoon olive oil
2 pounds ground turkey
1½ teaspoons ground cumin
1½ teaspoons dried oregano
1½ teaspoons onion powder
1½ teaspoons garlic powder
½ teaspoon freshly ground black pepper
1 teaspoon kosher salt
2 red bell peppers, cored and diced
2 tablespoons tomato paste
1 tablespoon apple cider vinegar
2 (15.5-ounce) cans red kidney beans, drained and rinsed; or 10 ounces dry red kidney beans, soaked and cooked
2 cups low-sodium chicken broth

1 cup jasmine rice

Directions
1. Season the turkey with ground cumin, dried oregano, onion powder, garlic powder, freshly ground black pepper, and kosher salt. Set aside for 15 minutes to marinate.
2. In a medium saucepan or skillet, heat oil over medium heat.
3. Add the turkey and cook until evenly browned about 5-6 minutes.
4. Add the bell peppers and cook for 2 minutes.
5. Create a pocket in the center of the mixture, then pour the vinegar and tomato paste into the pocket. Stir gently and cook for 30 seconds.
6. Add in the beans, rice, and broth. Stir until everything is well-combined.
7. Bring to a boil.
8. Over low heat, cover and simmer for about 40-45 minutes or until rice is tender.
9. Serve whilst warm.

Nutrition:
Calories: 324, fat: 11g, carbs: 21g, protein: 27g, sodium: 384 mg

Beef and Bean One-Pot Rice

Preparation time: 10 minutes
Cooking time: 20 minutes
Servings: 6

Ingredients
- 1 tablespoon olive oil
- 1 large onion, chopped
- 2 cloves garlic, minced
- 1 pound ground beef
- 1 red bell pepper, cored and diced
- 1 yellow bell pepper, cored and diced
- 1 tablespoon tomato paste
- 1 tablespoon taco seasoning
- Freshly ground black pepper and kosher salt, to taste
- 1 cup sweet corn, either canned or frozen and thawed
- 1 cup parboiled rice
- 1 ½ cups low-sodium broth of your choice
- 1 (16-ounce) jar chunky salsa
- 1 (15-ounce) can black beans, drained and rinsed; or 5 ounces dry black beans, soaked and cooked

Optional toppings:
Shredded cheese, chopped tomatoes, cilantro, lime wedges, sour cream, avocado, and tortilla chips

Directions
1. In a medium saucepan or skillet, heat oil over medium heat.
2. Add in the onion and cook until softened and translucent, about 2 minutes.
3. Add the garlic and beef. Cook until the meat is evenly browned.
4. Add both bell peppers and cook for 1 minute.
5. Add in the taco seasoning, tomato paste, freshly ground black pepper, and kosher salt and cook for another minute.
6. Add the corn, rice, broth, salsa, and beans. Stir gently to combine.
7. Over low heat, cover and simmer for about 15 minutes or until rice is cooked through. Add more broth if needed.
8. Top with the cheese and cook for 2 more minutes or until the cheese melts.
9. Serve with your choice of toppings.

Nutrition:
Calories: 385, fat: 7g, carbs: 55g, protein: 26g, sodium: 877 mg

Cannellini Bean Lamb Casserole

Preparation time: 10 minutes
Cooking time: 1½ hours
Servings: 4

Ingredients
- 28-ounce lamb shoulder, trimmed of fat and diced
- 3 tablespoons olive oil
- 1 large onion, thinly sliced
- 2 carrots, peeled and diced
- 2 stalks celery, diced
- 2 cloves garlic, crushed
- 1 teaspoon fresh rosemary, finely chopped
- 1 (14-ounce) can diced tomatoes with their juices
- 1 (14-ounce) can cannellini beans, drained and rinsed; or 5 ounces dry cannellini beans, soaked and cooked
- 1 large zucchini, trimmed and diced
- 2 medium-sized sweet potatoes, peeled and chopped
- Steamed green beans for serving

Directions
1. Preheat the oven to 325F (160C).
2. In a skillet or Dutch oven, heat 2 tablespoons of oil over medium heat.

3. Add the lamb and cook until evenly browned about 2-3 minutes. Set aside.
4. Add the remaining oil, celery, carrots, and onion. Cook until softened, about 4-5 minutes.
5. Add the rosemary and garlic. Cook for 1 minute or until fragrant.
6. Return the lamb to the pan. Add the tomatoes and 1½ cups water, then stir to combine.
7. Bring to a boil, then bake in the oven for 1 hour.
8. Add the zucchini, potatoes, and beans. Stir and bake for another 30 minutes or until lamb is tender.
9. Remove half the potatoes and mash them in a medium bowl.
10. Serve the casserole warm with steamed green beans and mashed potatoes.

Nutrition:
Calories: 628, fat: 26g, carbs: 34g, protein: 44g, sodium: 299mg

Zucchini Pinto Bean Casserole

Preparation time: 10 minutes
Cooking time: 20 minutes
Servings: 4

Ingredients
- 2 medium zucchinis, thinly and diagonally sliced
- Kosher salt, to taste
- 1 (15-ounce) can pinto beans, drained and rinsed; or 5 ounces dry pinto beans, soaked and cooked
- 1 cup prepared home-style salsa or pico de gallo salsa
- 1 tablespoon whole oregano leaves
- 6 (6-inch) corn tortillas, halved
- 1 cup Monterey Jack or Chihuahua cheese, shredded
- 2 tablespoons cilantro, chopped
- Lime wedges, to serve

Directions
1. Season the zucchini slices with ½ teaspoon kosher salt.
2. In a medium mixing bowl, add the oregano leaves, beans, and salsa. Mix until well-combined.
3. Preheat the oven to 375F (190C). Line a 9-inch baking pan or pie pan with parchment paper or foil.
4. Arrange 4 tortilla halves on the bottom of the pan, then add ⅓ of the bean mixture and ⅓ of the zucchini along with ¼ cup of the cheese.
5. Repeat layers and then top with kosher salt and the remaining cheese.
6. Bake for 15-20 minutes or until the cheese is melted and bubbling.
7. Remove from the over and top with the cilantro.

8. Serve with some lime wedges.

Nutrition:
Calories: 332, fat: 11g, carbs: 45g, protein: 14g, sodium: 106 mg

Chicken Bean Casserole

Preparation time: 15-20 minutes
Cooking time: 35 minutes
Servings: 12

Ingredients
- 1 large onion, chopped
- 1 large green bell pepper, chopped
- 2 cloves garlic, chopped
- 1 teaspoon kosher salt
- 1 teaspoon freshly ground black pepper
- 1 tablespoon ground cumin
- 1 teaspoon crushed red pepper flakes
- 1 (28-ounce) can diced tomatoes with their juices
- 2 (15-ounce) cans black beans, drained and rinsed; or 10 ounces dry black beans, soaked and cooked
- 1 (15-ounce) can chunky salsa
- 1 lb. boneless, skinless chicken breasts, chopped into bite-sized pieces
- 8-10 flour tortillas, halved
- 4 cups Mexican-blend cheese, shredded

For garnishing:
Tomatoes, chopped lettuce, and sour cream

Directions
1. In a medium saucepan or skillet, heat oil over medium heat.
2. Add the bell pepper, onion, and garlic. Cook until softened and translucent, about 4-5 minutes.
3. Add the kosher salt, freshly ground black pepper, ground cumin, and crushed red pepper flakes. Stir gently to combine.
4. Add the tomatoes, beans, salsa, and chicken. Mix until well-combined.
5. Simmer over low heat for 10 minutes, then set aside.
6. Preheat the oven to 350°F (175°C). Grease a 9x13 baking dish with cooking spray or cooking oil.
7. Arrange ⅓ of the tortilla halves on the bottom of the baking dish, then top with 1 cup of cheese and ⅓ of the bean mixture.
8. Repeat the layers twice more. Top with the remaining cheese.
9. Cover with foil and bake for about 35 minutes or until the cheese is melted and bubbling.
10. Serve with tomatoes, chopped lettuce, and sour cream.

Nutrition:
Calories: 444, fat: 20g, carbs: 42g, protein: 24g, sodium: 115mg

Beefy Bean Chili

Preparation time: 10 minutes
Cooking time: 50 minutes
Servings: 6

Ingredients
1 tablespoon olive oil
2 large red onions, chopped
5 tablespoons jalapeños with their seeds, chopped
8 garlic cloves, chopped
2⅓ pounds ground beef (15% fat)
1 teaspoon sweet paprika
2 tablespoons ground cumin
¼ cup chili powder
1 (28-ounce) can diced tomatoes with their juices
2 (15-ounce) cans kidney beans, drained and rinsed; or 10 ounces dry kidney beans, soaked and cooked
1 (14-ounce) can low-sodium beef broth

For toppings:
Grated cheddar cheese
Sour cream
Chopped green onions,
Chopped cilantro

Directions:
1. In a medium to large stockpot/deep saucepan/Dutch oven, heat oil over medium heat.
2. Add the onions and cook until softened and translucent, about 5-6 minutes.
3. Add the garlic and cook until fragrant, about 1 minute.
4. Add the beef and cook until evenly browned for about 4-5 minutes, then break into smaller pieces using a spatula.
5. Add the paprika, ground cumin, chili powder, beans, diced tomatoes with their juices, and broth. Stir to combine and bring to a boil.
6. Over low heat, simmer for about 45 minutes until the mixture thickens, stirring occasionally.
7. Top with the grated cheddar cheese, sour cream, chopped green onions, and chopped cilantro, then serve warm.

Nutrition:
Calories: 556, fat: 22g, carbs: 42g, protein: 49g, sodium: 674mg

Corn Mixed Bean Chili

Preparation time: 10 minutes
Cooking time: 1 hour 5-10 minutes
Servings: 12

Ingredients
For the chili:
- 2 large onions, chopped
- ¼ cup olive oil
- Freshly ground black pepper and kosher salt, to taste
- ½ cup tomato paste
- 1 teaspoon chipotle chili powder
- ¼ cup ancho chili powder
- 1 teaspoon ground coriander
- 1 teaspoon ground cumin
- ½ teaspoon cayenne pepper
- 4 cloves garlic, chopped
- 6 cups low-sodium vegetable broth
- 1 (28-ounce) can diced tomatoes with their juices
- 2 teaspoons Worcestershire sauce
- 1 (15-ounce) can black beans, drained and rinsed; or 5 ounces dry black beans, soaked and cooked
- 1 (15-ounce) can garbanzo beans, drained and rinsed; or 5 ounces dry garbanzo beans, soaked and cooked
- 1 (15-ounce) can kidney beans, drained and rinsed; or 5 ounces dry kidney beans, soaked and cooked
- 1 (15-ounce) can pinto beans, drained and rinsed; or 5 ounces dry pinto beans, soaked and cooked
- 2 cups canned corn

Optional toppings:
Sour cream, cooked crumbled bacon, chopped yellow onions, sliced jalapenos, chopped chives, corn chips, Greek yogurt, shredded cheddar cheese, and/or tortilla chips

Directions
1. In a medium/large Dutch oven, heat 2 tablespoons of oil over medium heat.
2. Add the onions, a pinch of freshly ground black pepper, and a pinch of kosher salt. Cook until softened and translucent, about 2-3 minutes.
3. Add the remaining oil, tomato paste, chipotle chili powder, ancho chili powder, ground cumin, ground coriander, cayenne pepper, and garlic. Cook for 1-2 minutes.
4. Add the Worcestershire sauce, beans, broth, tomatoes, corn, and 1 tablespoon kosher salt. Stir gently.

5. Simmer for about an hour until the mixture thickens, stirring occasionally.
6. Serve warm with your choice of toppings.

Nutrition:
Calories: 225, fat: 8g, carbs: 26g, protein: 13g, sodium: 987 mg

Shrimp Bean Chili

Preparation time: 5-10 minutes
Cooking time: 35 minutes
Servings: 4

Ingredients
- 1 tablespoon olive oil
- 1 small onion, chopped
- 1 jalapeno pepper, seeded and chopped
- 4 cloves garlic, chopped
- 2 tablespoons hot sauce of your choice
- 1 teaspoon ground cumin
- ½ teaspoon dried basil
- 1 (15-ounce) can red kidney beans, drained and rinsed; or 5 ounces dry red kidney beans, soaked and cooked
- 1 (15-ounce) can tomato sauce
- 2 Roma tomatoes, diced
- ¾ cup tomato paste
- 2 cups low-sodium chicken broth
- 1 tablespoon chili powder
- 1 lb. raw shrimp, peeled and deveined
- Cooked rice, to serve, optional

Directions:
1. In a medium/large saucepan or skillet, heat oil over medium heat.
2. Add in the onion and jalapeno. Cook until softened and translucent, about 4-5 minutes.
3. Add the garlic and cook until fragrant, about one minute.
4. Add the beans, hot sauce, basil, cumin, tomatoes, tomato paste, broth, and chili powder.
5. Over low heat, simmer for about 20 minutes until you achieve your desired consistency.
6. Add the shrimp and simmer until cooked through about 10 minutes.
7. Serve warm.

Nutrition:
Calories: 241, fat: 6g, carbs: 20g, protein 28g, sodium: 241 mg

Cheesy Mexican Lasagna

Preparation time: 15-20 minutes
Cooking time: 60 minutes
Servings: 12

Ingredients
- 2 tablespoons olive oil
- 4 cloves garlic, minced
- 1 cup sweet onion, diced
- 2 jalapeno peppers, seeded and diced
- 1 red bell pepper, cored and diced
- 1 (15.5-ounce) can black beans, drained and rinsed; or 5 ounces dry black beans, soaked and cooked
- 1 (16-ounce) jar salsa
- 1 (15 ¼-ounce) can whole-kernel corn, drained
- 1 teaspoon chili powder
- 1 teaspoon ground cumin
- 1 (10-ounce) package frozen chopped spinach, thawed and drained
- 1 large egg, beaten
- 2 cups ricotta cheese
- 3 cups Pepper Jack cheese, shredded
- ½ teaspoon kosher salt
- ½ teaspoon freshly ground black pepper
- 18 corn tortillas
- 1 cup enchilada sauce

Directions
1. Preheat the oven to 350°F (175°C). Grease a 9x13 baking dish with cooking spray or cooking oil.
2. In a large saucepan or skillet, heat oil over medium heat.
3. Add the garlic, onion, jalapenos, and bell pepper. Cook for 6-7 minutes until softened and translucent.
4. Reduce heat to low, then add the beans, salsa, corn, ground cumin, and chili powder. Simmer for about 5 minutes.
5. In a medium mixing bowl, combine the spinach, egg, 2 cups Pepper Jack cheese, ricotta cheese, freshly ground black pepper, and kosher salt.
6. In the baking dish, arrange 6 tortillas on the bottom. On top, add half the vegetable mixture, then add half the spinach mixture over the vegetable mixture.
7. Arrange 6 tortillas over the vegetable mixture, and top with the remaining vegetable and spinach mixture.

8. Finally, place the remaining tortillas on top. Top with the enchilada sauce and remaining Pepper Jack cheese.
9. Bake for 45-60 minutes or until the cheese is bubbly.
10. Slice and serve warm.

Nutrition:
Calories 411, fat 21 g, carbs 40 g, Protein 19.5 g, sodium 863 mg

Feta Bean Shakshuka

Preparation time: 10 minutes
Cooking time: 25 minutes
Servings: 4

Ingredients
- 1 teaspoon coriander seeds
- 1 teaspoon cumin seeds
- 1 teaspoon fennel seeds
- 2 tablespoons olive oil
- 1 red bell pepper, cored and thinly sliced
- 1 large yellow onion, thinly sliced
- 1 teaspoon smoked paprika
- 1 teaspoon kosher salt
- 1 (28-ounce) can diced tomatoes with their juices
- 1 (15-ounce) can white beans, drained and rinsed; or 5 ounces dry white beans, soaked and cooked
- 4-6 large eggs
- Freshly ground black pepper, to taste
- ½ cup cilantro leaves or flat-leaf parsley, chopped
- ½ cup feta cheese, crumbled

Directions
1. Heat a skillet over medium heat. Add the cumin, coriander, and fennel seeds. Toast for 2 minutes, then pour into a mortar and pestle. Grind the seeds until you achieve a powdery texture.
2. In a medium saucepan or skillet, heat oil over medium heat.
3. Add the onion and bell pepper. Cook for 3-4 minutes without stirring until lightly charred. Then cook until softened and translucent, about 5-6 more minutes.
4. Add the smoked paprika, kosher salt, and ground spices.
5. Add the diced tomatoes with their juices and stir well. Cook for a minute, and then boil the mixture over high heat.
6. Bring to low heat and simmer until the tomatoes have thickened, about 5 minutes.
7. Make four to six pockets in the mixture and crack the eggs in each of them.

8. Cover and cook for 4-6 minutes until eggs are set.
9. Serve warm with the cilantro leaves or parsley and top with the feta cheese.

Nutrition:
Calories: 292, fat: 19g, carbs: 18g, protein: 13.5g, sodium: 756 mg

Bean Turkey Quinoa Bake

Preparation time: 15 minutes
Cooking time: 30 minutes
Servings: 4-6

Ingredients
- 1 cup quinoa, uncooked
- 2 cups water
- Kosher salt, to taste
- 2 tablespoons extra-virgin olive oil
- 2 cups yellow onion, chopped
- 2 bell peppers, cored and chopped
- 1 teaspoon ground cumin
- 1 teaspoon chili powder, or to taste
- 4 cloves garlic, minced
- 1 cup frozen corn, thawed and drained
- 1 (15-ounce) can black beans, drained and rinsed; or 5 ounces dry black beans, soaked and cooked
- 3 cups cooked turkey, shredded and chopped
- 3 cups cheddar cheese, grated
- ½ cup cilantro, chopped

Directions
1. In a medium pot or saucepan, boil 2 cups of water. Add the quinoa and a pinch of kosher salt. Simmer over low heat for about 15 minutes until quinoa is cooked through. Remove from heat and fluff the quinoa using a fork.
2. In a medium saucepan or skillet, heat oil over medium heat.
3. Add the onion and bell peppers. Cook for 8-10 minutes until softened and the edges start to become brown.
4. Add the ground cumin, chili powder, garlic, and corn. Cook for 1 minute and then remove from heat.
5. In a large mixing bowl, add the beans, turkey, quinoa, onion mixture, 2 cups of cheddar cheese, and the cilantro. Toss to combine.
6. Preheat the oven to 350F (175C).

7. In a 9 by 13 baking dish, add the bean mixture and top with the remaining cheese. Bake uncovered until the cheese is bubbly, about 15 minutes.
8. Serve warm.

Nutrition:
Calories: 495, fat: 22g, carbs: 52g, protein: 24g, sodium: 108mg

Chapter 4: Soups

Cannellini Beef Soup

Preparation time: 20-30 minutes
Cooking time: 2 hours
Servings: 8

Ingredients
- 2 tablespoons canola oil
- 2 pounds beef stew meat, trimmed of fat and cut into 1-inch pieces
- 2 cups yellow onion, chopped
- 2 cups carrot, peeled and sliced/chopped
- 4 garlic cloves, minced
- 3 (15-ounce) cans cannellini beans, drained and rinsed; or 15 ounces dry cannellini beans, soaked and cooked
- 32 ounces or 4 cups low-sodium beef broth
- 2 cups water
- 1½ teaspoons kosher salt
- 1 teaspoon freshly ground black pepper
- 1 teaspoon dried thyme
- ½ teaspoon dried sage
- 4 bay leaves

Directions
1. In a medium to large stockpot/deep saucepan, heat 1 tablespoon of the oil over medium heat.
2. Add the meat and cook until evenly browned and set aside.
3. Add the remaining oil, garlic, onion, and carrot. Cook until veggies soften, about 4-5 minutes.
4. Add the meat, beans, broth, and water. Then add the thyme, sage, freshly ground black pepper, kosher salt, and bay leaves.
5. Over medium-low heat, cover and simmer for 1½ hours to 2 hours until the meat turns tender.
6. Remove the bay leaves, then add freshly ground black pepper and salt to taste.
7. Serve warm.

Nutrition:
Calories 433, fat: 21g, carbs: 24 g, protein: 30g, sodium: 601mg

Chorizo Bean Soup

Preparation time: 10-15 minutes
Cooking time: 35 minutes
Servings: 5-6

Ingredients
- 1 pound chorizo link sausage, casings removed
- 2 tablespoons olive oil
- 1 large yellow onion, chopped
- 3 garlic cloves, minced
- 1 teaspoon paprika
- 1 teaspoon kosher salt
- 2 medium carrots, peeled and chopped
- ½ pound small red potatoes, chopped
- 1 tablespoon tomato paste
- 2 (15-ounce) cans Great Northern beans, drained and rinsed; or 10 ounces dry Great Northern beans, soaked and cooked
- 1 (32-ounce) container low-sodium chicken broth
- ½ cup flat-leaf parsley, chopped

Directions
1. In a medium to large stockpot/deep saucepan/Dutch oven, heat half the oil over medium heat.
2. Add the chorizo and cook until evenly browned, about 7-8 minutes. Drain over a plate lined with a paper towel.
3. Wipe out the stockpot/deep saucepan/Dutch oven, then heat the remaining oil over medium heat.
4. Add in the onion, garlic, paprika, kosher salt, potatoes, and carrots. Cook until veggies soften, about 4-5 minutes.
5. Add the tomato paste and cook for 1 minute.
6. Add in the chorizo, beans, and broth, then bring to a boil.
7. Over medium-low heat, simmer the mixture for about 20 minutes.
8. Top with the flat-leaf parsley and serve warm.

Nutrition:
Calories: 424, fat: 18g, carbs: 27g, protein: 23g, sodium: 102mg

Spinach White Bean Soup

Preparation time: 10 minutes
Cooking time: 25 minutes
Servings: 6

Ingredients

- 1 tablespoon olive oil
- 1 large onion, chopped
- 2-3 celery stalks, chopped
- 2 garlic cloves, minced
- 2-3 large carrots, peeled and chopped
- 6 cups low-sodium vegetable broth
- 1 teaspoon dried thyme
- ½ teaspoon dried oregano
- 1 teaspoon kosher salt
- ½ teaspoon freshly ground black pepper
- 3 (15-ounce) cans white beans, drained and rinsed; or 15 ounces dry white beans, soaked and cooked
- 2 cups baby spinach
- Grated parmesan cheese and finely chopped flat-leaf parsley, for serving

Directions

1. In a medium to large stockpot/deep saucepan/Dutch oven, heat oil over medium heat.
2. Add the onion and cook until softened and translucent, about 3-5 minutes.
3. Add the celery, garlic, carrots, thyme, oregano, freshly ground black pepper, and kosher salt. Cook for 2-3 more minutes.
4. Add the broth and beans, then bring to a boil.
5. Over low heat, simmer the mixture for about 15 minutes.
6. Add the baby spinach. Cook for 2 minutes or until wilted.
7. Top with parmesan cheese and parsley.
8. Serve warm.

Nutrition:

Calories: 295, fat: 3g, carbs: 52g, protein: 17g, sodium: 415mg

Northern Bean Bacon Soup

Preparation time: 15 minutes
Cooking time: 35 minutes
Servings: 8

Ingredients

- 8 ounces thick-cut bacon, diced
- 1 cup yellow onion, diced
- 1 cup carrots, peeled and diced
- ¾ cup celery, diced
- 1 clove garlic, minced
- 2 tablespoons tomato paste
- 2 bay leaves

- 4 cups low-sodium chicken broth
- 3 cups water
- 3 (15-ounce) cans Great Northern beans, drained and rinsed; or 15 ounces dry Great Northern beans, soaked and cooked
- 1 teaspoon fresh chopped thyme or ½ teaspoon dried thyme
- 1 teaspoon kosher salt
- ¼ teaspoon freshly ground black pepper

Directions
1. In a medium/large saucepan or skillet, add the bacon and cook over medium heat until evenly crisped and browned. Drain the fat on a plate lined with a paper towel. Reserve 1 tablespoon of the bacon grease and discard the remaining grease.
2. Add the carrots, onion, celery, and garlic into the pan. Cook until softened, about 4-5 minutes.
3. Add the tomato paste and garlic. Cook for a minute or until fragrant.
4. Add half the cooked bacon, bay leaves, water, broth, beans, thyme, freshly ground black pepper and kosher salt. Bring to a boil.
5. Over medium-low heat, partially cover and simmer the mixture until softened, about 15-20 minutes.
6. Ladle half the soup into serving bowls and add the remaining soup to a blender. Blend until you get a puree-like texture.
7. Pour the blended soups into the serving bowls and top with the remaining bacon crumbles.
8. Serve warm.

Nutrition:
Calories: 158, fat: 12g, carbs: 7g, protein: 7g, sodium: 569mg

Chicken Spinach Bean Soup

Preparation time: 5 minutes
Cooking time: 15 minutes
Servings: 6

Ingredients
- 1 tablespoon extra-virgin olive oil
- 1 medium yellow onion, diced
- 1 pound ground chicken
- 1 clove garlic, minced
- 1 pinch crushed red pepper flakes
- ¼ teaspoon freshly ground black pepper
- 1 (14.5-ounce) can diced tomatoes and their juices
- 1 teaspoon dried oregano
- ½ teaspoon dried basil

- 1 (15.8-ounce) can Great Northern beans, drained and rinsed; or 5 ounces dry Great Northern beans, soaked and cooked
- 1 cup baby spinach
- 3 cups low-sodium chicken broth
- ½ cup parmesan cheese, grated

Directions

1. In a medium to large stockpot/deep saucepan/Dutch oven, heat oil over medium heat.
2. Add the onion, ground chicken, garlic, freshly ground black pepper, and crushed red pepper flakes. Cook until softened and translucent, about 6-7 minutes.
3. Add the diced tomatoes and their juices, oregano, basil, and beans. Combine well.
4. Add the spinach and simmer until wilted, about 2 minutes.
5. Add the broth and stir to combine. Cook for 4-5 minutes.
6. Divide the soup into serving bowls, top with the parmesan cheese, and serve warm.

Nutrition:

Calories: 268, fat: 8g, carbs: 17g, protein: 34g, sodium: 456 mg

Corn Black Bean Soup

Preparation time: 15 minutes
Cooking time: 30 minutes
Servings: 6

Ingredients

- 1 tablespoon olive oil
- 2 carrots, peeled and chopped
- 4 cloves garlic, chopped
- 1 large onion, chopped
- 1 stalk celery, chopped
- 1 tablespoon ground cumin
- 2 tablespoons chili powder
- 1 pinch freshly ground black pepper
- 4 cups low-sodium vegetable broth
- 1 (15-ounce) can whole-kernel corn
- 4 (15-ounce) cans black beans, drained and rinsed; or 20 ounces dry black beans, soaked and cooked
- 1 (14.5-ounce) can crushed tomatoes

Directions

1. In a medium to large stockpot/deep saucepan/Dutch oven, heat oil over medium heat.

2. Add the carrots, garlic, onion, and celery. Cook until softened and translucent, about 4-5 minutes.
3. Add the ground cumin, chili powder, and freshly ground black pepper. Cook for 1 minute.
4. Add the broth, corn, half the tomatoes, and half the beans. Bring to a boil, then simmer for about 15 minutes.
5. In the meantime, in a food processor or blender, add the remaining beans and tomatoes.
6. Blend until you get a smooth, rich mixture.
7. Add the mixture to the stockpot and stir to combine.
8. Serve warm.

Nutrition:
Calories: 410, fat: 5g, carbs: 75g, protein: 22g, sodium: 173mg

Italian Chicken Bean Soup

Preparation time: 15 minutes
Cooking time: 15 minutes
Servings: 6

Ingredients
- 2 teaspoons olive oil
- 3 stalks celery, sliced
- 3 carrots, peeled, quartered, and sliced
- 1 yellow onion, finely chopped
- 1 (14-ounce) can garlic and herb tomatoes (do not drain)
- 4 cups low-sodium chicken broth
- 2 zucchinis, quartered and sliced
- 1 (14-ounce) can red kidney beans, drained and rinsed; or 5 ounces dry red kidney beans, soaked and cooked
- 1 (14-ounce) can white beans, drained and rinsed; or 5 ounces dry white beans, soaked and cooked
- 4 cups chicken, cooked and shredded
- Freshly ground black pepper and salt, to taste
- 2 tablespoons flat-leaf parsley, chopped, optional

Directions
1. In a medium to large stockpot/deep saucepan/Dutch oven, heat oil over medium heat.
2. Add the carrots, celery, onion, freshly ground black pepper and kosher salt. Cook until softened, about 5-6 minutes.
3. Mix in the broth and tomatoes. Bring to a simmer.
4. Add the zucchini, beans, and chicken. Cook until zucchini turns tender, about 5-7 minutes.
5. Season to taste with freshly ground black pepper and kosher salt.
6. Top with the chopped parsley and serve warm.

Nutrition:
Calories: 286, fat: 14g, carbs: 21g, protein: 21g, sodium: 770mg

Lima Bean Ham Soup

Preparation time: 15 minutes
Cooking time: 35minutes
Servings: 6

Ingredients
- ¼ cup unsalted butter
- 1½ cups onion, chopped
- 1 cup carrots, peeled and diced
- 1 tablespoon lemon juice
- 1½ teaspoons garlic, minced or ½ teaspoon garlic powder
- 1 teaspoon Italian seasoning
- 3½ ounces baby lima beans, soaked and cooked
- 1½ cups ham, diced
- ½ cup flat-leaf parsley, chopped
- 2 teaspoons dried marjoram
- 4 cups unsalted chicken stock or vegetable stock (or water)
- Freshly ground black pepper and kosher salt, to taste

Directions
1. In a medium to large stockpot/deep saucepan/Dutch oven, heat butter over medium heat until melted.
2. Add the carrots and onion. Cook until softened and translucent, about 5-7 minutes.
3. Add the lemon juice, garlic, and Italian seasoning and cook for 2 minutes.
4. Add the beans, ham, parsley, and marjoram. Add the stock or water, then bring to a boil.
5. Over low heat, cover, and simmer for about 20 minutes.
6. Season to taste with freshly ground black pepper and salt.
7. Serve warm.

Nutrition:
Calories: 212, fat: 10g, carbs: 21g, protein: 12g, sodium: 677 mg

Corn Beef Bean Soup

Preparation time: 15 minutes
Cooking time: 6 hours
Servings: 8

Ingredients
- 1 tablespoon olive oil
- 2 pounds ground beef
- 1 yellow onion, chopped
- 2 cloves garlic, minced
- 4 carrots, peeled and chopped
- 2 stalks celery, chopped
- 2 cups low-sodium vegetable or chicken stock
- 1 (28-ounce) can crushed tomatoes
- 1 (15-ounce) can cannellini beans, drained and rinsed; or 5 ounces dry cannellini beans, soaked and cooked
- 2 cups frozen corn, thawed
- 1 tablespoon kosher salt
- ½ teaspoon freshly ground black pepper
- ¼ teaspoon dried thyme

Directions
1. Season the beef with half of the freshly ground black pepper and half of the kosher salt.
2. In a medium saucepan or skillet, heat the oil over medium heat.
3. Add the onion, ground beef, and garlic and cook until beef is evenly browned.
4. In a slow cooker, add the beef mixture, carrots, celery, stock, and tomatoes. Stir until everything is well-combined.
5. Add the beans, thyme, and remaining freshly ground black pepper and kosher salt. Stir well to combine.
6. Close the lid, ensure it's in the sealing position, and select the LOW setting. Set the timer for 5 hours.
7. When the time is up, open the lid, add the corn, and cook on the LOW setting for 1 hour.
8. Season to taste with more freshly ground black pepper and kosher salt.
9. Serve warm.

Nutrition:
Calories: 309, fat: 12g, carbs: 19g, protein: 27g, sodium 877 mg

Vegetarian Spiced Black Bean Soup

Preparation time: 15-20 minutes
Cooking time: 55 minutes
Servings: 8

Ingredients
- 2 tablespoons olive oil
- 1 yellow bell pepper, cored and diced
- 1 medium white onion, chopped

- 4 teaspoons chili powder
- 1½ teaspoons ground cumin
- 1½ teaspoons dried oregano
- 5 cloves garlic, minced
- ½ teaspoon kosher salt
- ½ teaspoon freshly ground black pepper
- ¼ teaspoon chipotle chili powder
- 6 cups low-sodium vegetable broth
- 1 lb. dry black beans, soaked and cooked
- 1 (4-ounce) can chopped Hatch chili peppers (do not drain)
- 1 pinch garlic salt, or to taste

For the garnish
- 1 red bell pepper, cored and sliced
- 1 cup pico de gallo salsa or homemade salsa
- Lime wedges, to serve

Directions
1. Add the oil to an Instant Pot or pressure cooker and select the SAUTE mode.
2. When the oil is hot, add the bell pepper and onion. Cook until translucent, about 4-5 minutes.
3. Add the cumin, chili powder, oregano, garlic, freshly ground black pepper, kosher salt, and chipotle chili powder. Cook until fragrant, about one minute.
4. Add the beans, broth, and chili peppers.
5. Close the lid and ensure it's in the sealing position. Select. the HIGH setting and set the timer to 40 minutes.
6. After the time is over, allow the. pressure to release naturally.
7. Transfer the soup to a blender or food processor. Blend until the soup is creamy.
8. Season to taste with garlic salt.
9. Serve warm with salsa, bell pepper, and lime wedges.

Nutrition:
Calories: 280, fat: 5g, carbs: 45g, protein: 14g, sodium: 870mg

Arugula Bean Potato Soup

Preparation time: 10 minutes
Cooking time: 35-40 minutes
Servings: 6

Ingredients
For the croutons:
- 2 tablespoons olive oil

- 4 cups Italian baguette, cubed
- ¼ cup parmesan cheese, grated
- Kosher salt and freshly ground black pepper, to taste

For the soup:
- 2 tablespoons olive oil
- 2 cups onions, diced
- 2 tablespoons fresh rosemary, minced
- 1 tablespoon garlic, minced
- ½ cup dry white wine
- 1 pound Yukon Gold potatoes, cubed
- 6 cups low-sodium chicken broth
- 1 can (15-ounce) cannellini beans, drained and rinsed; or 5 ounces dry cannellini beans, soaked and cooked
- 5 ounces arugula leaves
- Kosher salt, freshly ground black pepper and crushed red pepper flakes, to taste
- Extra-virgin olive oil, for drizzling

Directions
1. In a medium skillet, heat 1 tablespoon of oil over medium heat.
2. Add the baguette cubes and cook until toasted, about 4-5 minutes.
3. In a large mixing bowl, combine the baguette croutons with the parmesan cheese. Season to taste with freshly ground black pepper and kosher salt.
4. In a medium to large stockpot, deep saucepan or Dutch oven, heat 1 tablespoon of oil over medium heat.
5. Add the onions and cook until softened and translucent, about 4-5 minutes.
6. Add in the rosemary and garlic, then cook until fragrant, about 1 minute.
7. Add the wine and cook for 3 minutes until it evaporates.
8. Mix in the potatoes and broth, then bring to a boil.
9. Over medium-low heat, simmer the mixture for about 10-12 minutes or until the potatoes turn tender.
10. Add the arugula and beans. Simmer for about 2 minutes or until the arugula wilts.
11. Season to taste with crushed red pepper flakes, freshly ground black pepper, and kosher salt.
12. Divide into serving bowls, then top with the croutons and drizzle with olive oil.
13. Serve warm.

Nutrition:
Calories: 332, fat: 11g, carbs: 43g, protein: 19g, sodium: 345 mg

Veggie Bean Soup

Preparation time: 10 minutes
Cooking time: 35 minutes
Servings: 4

Ingredients
- 2 tablespoons extra-virgin olive oil
- 2 stalks celery, diced
- 2 medium carrots, peeled and diced
- 1 medium yellow onion, diced
- 3 garlic cloves, minced
- 1 teaspoon dried thyme
- Freshly ground black pepper and kosher salt, to taste
- 1 28-ounce can chopped tomatoes with their juices
- 2 (15.5-ounce) cans cannellini beans, drained and rinsed; or 10 ounces dry cannellini beans, soaked and cooked
- 4 cups low-sodium vegetable broth
- ¼ cup flat-leaf parsley, chopped
- Parmesan cheese, grated and to taste

Directions
1. In a medium to large stockpot, deep saucepan or Dutch oven, heat the oil over medium-high heat.
2. Add the celery, onion, and carrots. Cook until softened and translucent, about 5-6 minutes.
3. Add the thyme, garlic, freshly ground black pepper and kosher salt. Cook until fragrant, about 2-3 minutes.
4. Add the tomatoes, beans, parsley, and broth. Stir gently to combine, then bring to a boil.
5. Over medium-low heat, simmer the mixture for about 25-30 minutes or until the vegetables turn tender.
6. Season to taste with freshly ground black pepper and kosher salt. Top with Parmesan cheese.
7. Serve warm.

Nutrition:
Calories: 313, fat: 8g, carbs: 44g, protein: 13g, sodium: 117 mg

Parmesan Turkey Bean Soup

Preparation time: 20 minutes
Cooking time: 3 hours
Servings: 6

Ingredients
- 1 lb. dry white beans, soaked and cooked
- 2 smoked turkey legs
- ½ yellow onion, diced
- 2 bay leaves
- 2 stalks celery, diced
- 4 large carrots, peeled and sliced
- 1 (14.5-ounce) can diced tomatoes with their juices
- 2 tablespoons Italian seasoning
- Freshly ground black pepper and kosher salt, to taste
- 2 tablespoons parmesan cheese, grated

Directions
1. In a medium to large stockpot, deep saucepan or Dutch oven, heat the oil over medium heat.
2. Add the onion and cook until softened and translucent.
3. Add the turkey legs and bay leaves. Add water until it just covers the turkey legs, then bring to a boil.
4. Over low heat, simmer the mixture for about 2 hours. Discard the bay leaves.
5. Take out the turkey legs and remove the meat from the bones.
6. Add the meat back to the pot, then add the beans, carrots, celery, Italian seasoning, freshly ground black pepper, and kosher salt. Stir well to combine.
7. Over low heat, simmer the mixture for about 1 hour or until the. vegetables become tender.
8. Top with parmesan cheese and serve warm.

Nutrition:
Calories: 454, fat: 9g, carbs: 54g, protein: 40g, sodium: 938 mg

Tuscan Bean and Chicken Soup

Preparation time: 15 minutes
Cooking time: 45 minutes
Servings: 4

Ingredients
- 1 tablespoon olive oil
- 1 yellow onion, chopped

- 2 cloves garlic, minced
- ½ teaspoon dried thyme or 2 sprigs fresh thyme
- 2 medium carrots, peeled and chopped
- 1 stalk celery, sliced
- 2 medium potatoes, peeled and diced
- 4 cups low-sodium chicken stock
- ½ teaspoon kosher salt
- ½ teaspoon freshly ground black pepper
- 1 (15-ounce) can cannellini beans, drained and rinsed; or 5 ounces dry cannellini beans, soaked and cooked
- 2 skinless cooked chicken breasts, shredded
- 3 ½ ounces kale, stemmed and chopped
- Small bunch flat-leaf parsley, chopped
- 2 tablespoons parmesan cheese, finely grated
- Toasted bread and fresh thyme leaves, to serve

Directions

1. In a large stockpot, deep saucepan or Dutch oven, heat oil over medium-low heat.
2. Add the onion and cook until softened and translucent, about 10 minutes.
3. Add the thyme and garlic. Cook until fragrant, about 1-2 minutes.
4. Add the carrots, celery, and potatoes. Add the chicken stock, freshly ground black pepper, and kosher salt, then bring to a boil.
5. Over low heat, simmer the mixture for about 20 minutes.
6. Add the beans and cook for 4-5 minutes.
7. Add the chicken and cook for 2-3 more minutes.
8. Add the kale and simmer for 1-2 minutes or until wilted.
9. Season with more freshly ground black pepper and kosher salt to taste.
10. Divide the soup into serving bowls, then top with the parmesan cheese, parsley, and thyme.
11. Serve warm with the toasted bread.

Nutrition:
Calories: 412, fat: 9g, carbs: 52g, protein: 31g, sodium: 807mg

Sweet Potato Bean Soup

Preparation time: 10 minutes
Cooking time: 60 minutes
Servings: 6

Ingredients
- 2 tablespoons olive oil
- 1 medium onion, chopped
- 2-3 stalks celery, chopped

- ¼ teaspoon ground nutmeg
- 1 teaspoon ground turmeric
- 1 teaspoon kosher salt
- ½ teaspoon freshly ground black pepper
- 1 cup dry adzuki beans, soaked and cooked
- 2 medium sweet potatoes, coarsely chopped
- 1 cup kale, stemmed and torn into small pieces
- 6 cups water
- ½ cup flat-leaf parsley, chopped

Directions

1. In a medium to large stockpot/deep saucepan/Dutch oven, heat oil over medium heat.
2. Add the celery, onion, ground nutmeg, ground turmeric, and freshly ground black pepper. Cook until the onion has softened, about 4-5 minutes.
3. Add the water and beans, then bring to a boil over medium-high heat.
4. Simmer for 20 minutes.
5. Add the kale and potatoes, then bring to a boil again. Cook for about 30 minutes or until the potatoes are tender.
6. Season to taste with kosher salt, then top with the parsley.
7. Serve warm.

Nutrition:
Calories: 191, fat: 6g, carbs: 25g, protein: 5g, sodium: 558mg

Black Bean Soup

Preparation time: 15 minutes
Cooking time: 2 hours and 10 minutes
Servings: 5
Ingredients:
- 1 lb. black beans, dried
- 4 carrots, diced
- 2 onions, one-finely diced, one-halved
- 1 poblano pepper, seeded, diced
- 3 garlic cloves, minced
- 2 cups ham, diced
- 10 cups chicken stock
- 2 tsp cumin, ground
- 1½ tsp black pepper, freshly ground
- 3 tsp kosher salt
- 2 tsp oregano
- ½ tsp cayenne pepper

Directions:
1. In a large bowl, add the washed beans and soak in 3 inches of water. Drain and then rinse.
2. Put the beans in a pot. Pour in about 3 inches of cold water. Add the halved onion and bring it to a boil on high heat.
3. Reduce the heat and let it simmer for 30 minutes. Strain the beans and discard the liquid and onion. Set aside.
4. In another pot, mix the stock and all the remaining ingredients. Let it simmer until thoroughly heated. Strain the mixture, reserve both stock and vegetables.
5. In each hot jar, fill ¼ of the jars with beans, ¼ cup vegetables, and ham. Pour stock over them. Leave a space of 1-inch at the top. Remove the air bubbles.
6. Clean the rim of the glass jar. Screw on the lid and apply a band around it. Ensure that the lid is secured tightly.
7. In a pressure canner, place the jars on the racks with simmering water (2-inches, 900C/1800F).
8. Close the lid of the canner and adjust to medium-high heat. Vent steam for 10 minutes at 10/11 pounds (psi for weighted gauge/dial-gauge canner). Process pint jars for 75 minutes or quarts for 90 minutes.
9. Turn off the canner, open the lid after two minutes when the pressure reaches zero. Keep the jars in the canner for 10 minutes more.
10. Remove the jars. Reprocess if the jars are not sealed. Cool and store in the refrigerator.

Nutrition: Calories: 110, carbs: 60g, fat: 2g, protein: 6g

Chapter 5: Bread and Flour

Bean Salsa with Tortilla Chips

Preparation time: 10 minutes
Cooking time: 5 minutes
Servings: 12

Ingredients

- 1 (15-ounce) can whole-kernel corn, drained
- ½ cup yellow onion, chopped
- 1 (15-ounce) can black-eyed peas, drained and rinsed; or 5 ounces dry black-eyed peas, soaked and cooked
- 1 (15-ounce) can black beans, drained and rinsed; or 5 ounces dry black beans, soaked and cooked
- ½ cup green bell pepper, cored and chopped
- 1 (4-ounce) can diced jalapeno peppers
- 1 (14.5-ounce) can diced tomatoes, drained
- 1 cup Italian-style salad dressing
- ½ teaspoon garlic salt

For the tortilla chips
- 6 (7½ inches each) flour tortillas, cut into 8 wedges
- Cooking spray or olive oil for greasing

Directions

1. In a large mixing bowl, add the corn, onion, beans, black-eyed peas, bell pepper, jalapeno peppers, and diced tomatoes and mix well.
2. Add the salad dressing and garlic salt and combine.
3. Refrigerate for 8 hours or overnight for the flavors to blend.
4. Preheat the oven on the BROIL setting. Grease a baking dish with cooking spray or cooking oil.
5. Arrange the tortilla wedges on the baking dish and broil for 1-2 minutes. Flip the wedges and broil for 1-2 minutes or until evenly browned.
6. Serve the tortilla chips with the prepared bean salsa.

Nutrition:
Calories: 155, fat: 6.5g, carbs: 20.5g, protein: 5g, sodium: 948mg

Cheesy Black Bean Nachos

Preparation time: 5 minutes
Cooking time 10 minutes
Servings: 4

Ingredients
- 1 (15-ounce) can black beans, drained and rinsed; or 5 ounces dry black beans, soaked and cooked
- 1 (14.5-ounce) can diced tomatoes, drained
- 3-4 jalapeno peppers, seeded and sliced
- 4 cups multigrain tortilla chips
- 1 cup cheddar cheese, shredded

Optional toppings:
Chopped cilantro, sour cream, and sliced jalapeno

Directions
1. Preheat the oven to 350°F (175°C). Grease a baking dish or baking sheet with cooking spray or cooking oil.
2. In a medium mixing bowl, combine the beans, tomatoes, and jalapenos.
3. Arrange the tortilla chips on the bottom of the baking dish. Top with the bean mixture and cheddar cheese.
4. Bake for 10-12 minutes or until the cheese is melted.
5. Serve warm with the toppings of your choice.

Nutrition:
Calories: 371, fat: 17g, carbs: 42 g, protein: 15g, sodium: 672mg

Bean Toasts

Preparation time: 5 minutes
Cooking time: 5 minutes
Servings: 4

Ingredients
- 2 tablespoons unsalted butter
- 1 cup spring onion, chopped (whites only)
- 1½ tablespoons garlic, minced
- 1 medium bell pepper, chopped
- 2 cup baked beans
- 2½ tablespoons crushed red pepper flakes
- 2½ tablespoons ketchup
- 2 teaspoons dried oregano
- Kosher salt, to taste
- 4 bread slices, toasted

- 1 bunch cilantro, chopped
- Grated cheese of choice, optional

Directions
1. In a medium saucepan or skillet, heat the butter over medium heat until melted.
2. Add the spring onion and garlic, then cook until translucent and softened.
3. Add the bell pepper and cook for 1-2 minutes.
4. Mix in the beans, crushed red pepper flakes, ketchup, oregano, and salt. Cook for 2-3 minutes.
5. Spoon the bean mixture evenly over the toasted bread slices.
6. Add the cilantro and grated cheese evenly over the bean mixture on each slice.
7. Serve warm.

Nutrition:
Calories: 274, fat: 8g, carbs 43g, protein: 9g, sodium: 785mg

Black Bean Burger

Preparation time: 15 minutes
Cooking time: 20 minutes
Servings: 4

Ingredients
- 1 (16-ounce) can black beans, drained and rinsed; or 5 ounces dry black beans, soaked and cooked
- ½ green bell pepper, cored and cut into 2-inch pieces
- ½ yellow onion, cut into wedges
- 3 cloves garlic, peeled
- 1 large egg
- 1 tablespoon chili powder
- 1 tablespoon ground cumin
- 1 teaspoon Thai chili sauce or hot sauce
- ½ cup breadcrumbs

To serve
Burger buns and toppings (tomato slices, shredded lettuce, ketchup, BBQ sauce, mayonnaise, etc.)

Directions
1. Using a spatula, mash the beans in a large mixing bowl until you get a thick consistency.
2. In a blender or food processor, add the garlic, bell pepper, and onion.
3. After blending, mix the garlic mixture with the beans in the mixing bowl.

4. In another medium mixing bowl, add the egg, ground cumin, chili powder, and chili sauce.
5. Add the egg mixture to the bean mixture along with the breadcrumbs. Combine until smooth.
6. Using your hands, form 4 burger patties from the mixture.
7. Preheat the grill over medium heat and grease the grates with some vegetable oil.
8. Grill the patties on both sides until evenly browned.
9. On the bottom burger bun, arrange a burger patty followed by a cheese slice. Add the toppings of your choice and top with the top burger bun. Repeat with the other patties.
10. Serve warm.

Nutrition (per patty)
Calories: 198, fat: 3g, carbs: 33g, protein: 11g, sodium: 607mg

Avocado Bean Wrap

Preparation time: 10 minutes
Cooking time: 10 minutes
Servings: 6

Ingredients
Beans
- 1 tablespoon olive oil
- ½ cup yellow onion, chopped
- ½ cup bell pepper, cored and chopped, optional
- 1 clove garlic, minced
- 1 (15-ounce) can black beans, drained and rinsed; or 5 ounces dry black beans, soaked and cooked
- 1 tablespoon taco seasoning, or to make your own taco seasoning, combine ½ teaspoon chili powder, ¼ teaspoon garlic powder, ½ teaspoon cumin, ¼ teaspoon freshly ground black pepper, ½ teaspoon paprika, and ¼ teaspoon kosher salt

Avocado salsa
- 2 tablespoons cilantro, minced
- Juice of 1 lime
- 1 avocado, pitted and chopped
- 1 small tomato, chopped
- Freshly ground black pepper and kosher salt, to taste
- 6 medium tortillas
- ¼ cup mayonnaise, sour cream, or chipotle sauce

Directions

1. In a medium saucepan or skillet, heat the oil over medium heat.
2. Add the onion, bell pepper, and garlic. Cook until softened and golden, about 2-3 minutes.
3. Add the beans and taco seasoning. Cook for 2-3 minutes, then remove from heat.
4. In a medium mixing bowl, add the cilantro, lime juice, avocado, tomato, a pinch of freshly ground black pepper, and a pinch of kosher salt. Combine until well-mixed.
5. To make the wraps, arrange a tortilla and spoon mayonnaise/sour cream (about 1 teaspoon) in the center of the tortilla. Add the bean mixture and avocado salsa, then roll to seal the wrap. Repeat with remaining tortillas, bean mixture, and salsa.
6. Serve fresh.

Nutrition:

Calories: 428, fat: 12g, carbs: 61g, protein: 18g, sodium: 147 mg

Chapter 6: Snacks and Desserts

Black Bean Avocado Brownie

Preparation time: 10 minutes
Cooking time: 38 minutes
Servings: 9

Ingredients
1 (15-ounce) can black beans, drained and rinsed; or 5 ounces dry black beans, soaked and cooked
½ cup unsweetened cocoa powder
3 large eggs
¼ cup vegetable oil or melted coconut oil
¾ cup granulated sugar
¼ teaspoon kosher salt
1 teaspoon baking powder
1 teaspoon pure vanilla extract
1 medium avocado, pitted and peeled
1 cup dark chocolate chips

Directions
1. Preheat the oven to 350F (175C). Grease an 8 by 8 inch baking dish with cooking spray or cooking oil.
2. In a food processor or blender, add all the ingredients except the chocolate chips. Blend until you get a smooth, rich mixture.
3. Add the brownie mixture to the baking dish and top with the chocolate chips.
4. Bake for about 35-40 minutes or until a toothpick comes out clean.
5. Let cool for 10-15 minutes.
6. Slice and serve warm.
7. To store, refrigerate in an air-tight container for 4-5 days.

Nutrition (per brownie)
Calories: 212, fat: 15g, carbs: 32g, protein: 5.5g, sodium: 193mg

Bean Peanut Butter Blondies

Preparation time: 10 minutes
Cooking time: 20 minutes
Servings: 9

Ingredients

- 1 (15-ounce) can butter beans, drained and rinsed; or 5 ounces dry butter beans, soaked and cooked
- ⅓ cup honey or maple syrup
- ½ cup natural peanut butter
- ¼ teaspoon kosher salt
- 2 teaspoons vanilla extract
- ¼ teaspoon baking powder
- ¼ teaspoon baking soda
- ⅓ + ¼ cup dark chocolate chips

Directions

1. Preheat the oven to 350°F (175°C). Grease an 8 by 8 inch pie pan or baking dish with cooking spray or cooking oil.
2. In a food processor or blender, add the beans. Blend on pulse mode to puree the beans.
3. Add the honey/maple syrup, peanut butter, kosher salt, vanilla extract, baking soda, and baking powder.
4. Blend until you get a smooth, rich mixture.
5. Add ⅓ of the chocolate chips, then blend again.
6. Add the chocolate mixture to the pie pan/baking dish, then top with the remaining chocolate chips.
7. Bake for 20-25 minutes or until a toothpick comes out clean.
8. Let cool for 10-15 minutes.
9. Slice and serve warm.

Nutrition:
Calories: 221, fat: 10g, carbs: 27g, protein: 9g, sodium: 311mg

White Navy Bean Carrot Blondies

Preparation time: 10 minutes
Cooking time: 25 minutes
Servings: 9

Ingredients

- ½ cup old-fashioned oats
- ¼ cup creamy peanut butter
- ¼ teaspoon kosher salt
- ½ teaspoon baking powder
- ½ cup maple syrup
- 1 teaspoon pure vanilla extract
- 1 (15.5-ounce) can white navy beans, drained and rinsed; or 5 ounces dry white navy beans, soaked and cooked
- 1 cup carrots, peeled and shredded

- ¼ cup chocolate chips

Direction
1. Preheat the oven to 350°F (175°C). Grease an 8 by 8 inch pie pan or baking dish with cooking spray or cooking oil.
2. In a food processor or blender, add the oats. Blend on pulse mode until you get a flour-like consistency.
3. Add the peanut butter, kosher salt, baking powder, maple syrup, vanilla extract, beans, and carrots to the blender.
4. Blend until you get a smooth, rich mixture.
5. Add the mixture to the pie pan/baking dish, then top with the remaining chocolate chips. You can also add more shredded carrots on top if desired.
6. Bake until the edges start to brown, about 20-25 minutes.
7. Let cool for 10-15 minutes.
8. Slice into squares and serve warm. To store, refrigerate for up to 5-7 days in an air-tight container.

Nutrition:
Calories: 185, fat: 5g, carbs: 30g, protein: 6g, sodium: 114mg

Garbanzo Bean Chocolate Cake

Preparation time: 15 minutes
Cooking time: 40 minutes
Servings: 12

Ingredients
- 1 ½ cups semisweet chocolate chips
- 1 (19-ounce) can garbanzo beans, drained and rinsed; or 6 ounces dry garbanzo beans, soaked and cooked
- 4 large eggs
- ¾ cup granulated sugar
- ½ teaspoon baking powder
- 1 tablespoon confectioner's sugar

Direction
1. Preheat the oven to 350F (175C). Grease a 9-inch round cake pan or baking dish with cooking spray or cooking oil.
2. Melt the chocolate in the microwave or in a double boiler over medium-high heat. Melt for 2 minutes while stirring regularly.
3. In a food processor or blender, add the eggs and beans. Blend until you get a smooth, rich mixture.
4. Add the baking powder and sugar. Blend again.
5. Add the melted chocolate and blend until smooth.
6. Add the cake mix to the cake pan/baking dish. Bake for about 40 minutes or until a toothpick comes out clean.

7. Let cool for 10-15 minutes.
8. Dust with the confectioner's sugar, slice and serve warm.

Nutrition:
Calories 227, fat 8.5 g, carbs 37 g, Protein 5 g, sodium 180 mg

Black Bean Choco Truffles

Preparation time: 20 minutes
Cooking time: 30 seconds
Servings: 10

Ingredients
For the truffles:
- ¼ cup unsweetened cocoa powder
- ½ teaspoon pure vanilla extract
- 1 (15-ounce) can black beans, drained and rinsed; or 5 ounces dry black beans, soaked and cooked
- 1 ripe medium avocado, pitted and peeled
- ½ cup dark chocolate chips
- ½ teaspoon coconut oil

For the chocolate coating:
- 1 cup dark chocolate chips
- 1 teaspoon coconut oil
- Sea salt, to taste
- Shredded coconut, optional

Direction
1. In a food processor or blender, add the vanilla extract, cocoa powder, beans, and avocado.
2. Blend everything until you get a smooth, rich mixture.
3. Melt the chocolate chips and coconut oil in the microwave or in a double-boiler over medium-high heat. Melt for 2 minutes while stirring regularly.
4. Add the melted chocolate to the bean mixture. Mix until well-combined.
5. Add the mixture to a large bowl and refrigerate until the batter firms up, about 10-20 minutes.
6. Form truffle balls from the mixture (about 1-2 tablespoons of batter per truffle).
7. Arrange the truffles on a baking sheet lined with parchment paper. Refrigerate until they are well-set.
8. To make the coating, melt the chocolate chips and coconut oil in the microwave or in a. double boiler over medium-high heat. Melt for 2 minutes while stirring regularly.

9. Roll the truffles into the melted chocolate until they are covered evenly and arrange them on a baking sheet lined with parchment paper.
10. Sprinkle the sea salt and shredded coconut on top if desired. Refrigerate the truffles for 5 more minutes.
11. Serve chilled.

Nutrition:
Calories: 33, fat: 2g, carbs: 3g, protein: 1g, sodium: 73mg

Chocolate and Peanut Butter Bites

Preparation time: 10 minutes
Cooking time: 5 minutes
Servings: 12

Ingredients
For the dough:
- 1 (15.5-ounce) can chickpeas, drained and rinsed; or 5 ounces dry chickpeas, soaked and cooked
- 1 teaspoon pure vanilla extract
- 3 tablespoons maple syrup
- 1 tablespoon vegetable oil
- 2 tablespoons peanut butter powder
- ½ cup peanut butter, smooth or chunky
- ¼ teaspoon kosher salt
- ¼ cup chocolate chips

For the chocolate drizzle:
- ¼ cup chocolate chips
- ½ teaspoon coconut oil
- ¼ teaspoon sea salt, optional

Direction
1. Line a baking sheet with parchment paper.
2. In a food processor or blender, add the chickpeas. Blend on pulse mode until the chickpeas have completely broken down.
3. Add the vanilla extract, maple syrup, oil, powdered peanut butter, peanut butter, vanilla, and salt to the blender. Blend for about 1 minute until the mixture is smooth.
4. Add the mixture to a bowl and stir in the chocolate chips.
5. Refrigerate for about 5 minutes or until the batter firms up.
6. Roll into balls of around 1 inch.
7. Transfer the balls to the prepared baking sheet.
8. To make the chocolate drizzle, melt the chocolate chips and coconut oil in the microwave or in a double boiler over medium-high heat. Melt for 2 minutes while stirring regularly.

9. Drizzle the sauce over the prepared dough bites. Sprinkle sea salt on top, if desired.
10. Refrigerate for 5 more minutes, then serve chilled.

Nutrition:
Calories: 125, fat: 8g, carbs 11g, protein: 5g, sodium: 208mg

Walnut Bean Dip

Preparation time: 5 minutes
Cooking time: 0 minutes
Servings: 6

Ingredients
- 1 (15-ounce) can white beans, drained and rinsed; or 5 ounces dry white beans, soaked and cooked
- 1 tablespoon extra-virgin olive oil
- 2 tablespoons lime juice
- 1 canned Adobo chipotle pepper (do not drain sauce)
- Kosher salt, to taste
- 1-2 garlic cloves, smashed
- ½ cup California walnuts, chopped
- ⅓ cup lightly packed cilantro leaves

Directions
1. In a food processor or blender, add the beans, olive oil, salt, garlic, lime juice, chipotle pepper, and 2 tablespoons of the sauce from the canned chipotle.
2. Blend until you get a smooth, rich mixture.
3. Add the walnuts and cilantro, then blend until the walnuts are roughly chopped.
4. Add the mixture to a bowl and then cover and refrigerate to chill.

Nutrition:
Calories: 130, fat: 9g, carbs: 12g, protein: 4g, sodium: 320mg

Bacon Lima Bean Dip

Preparation time: 15 minutes
Cooking time: 20 minutes
Servings: 4-6

Ingredients
- ¼ cup loosely packed flat-leaf parsley
- Zest and juice of ½ lemon

- 1 (10-ounce) box frozen lima beans, thawed
- 2 cloves garlic, smashed
- ¼ cup extra-virgin olive oil
- 2½ teaspoons Kosher salt
- 2 slices bacon
- Vegetable sticks and pita chips, to serve

Directions

1. In a medium saucepan or skillet, add bacon and cook over medium heat until evenly crisp and brown. Drain over paper towels, discard the bacon grease, and crumble the bacon onto a plate.
2. In a deep saucepan, add water and 1 teaspoon of Kosher salt.
3. Add the lima beans and boil over medium-high heat for 18-20 minutes until they have softened. Drain and rinse the beans, then set aside to cool.
4. In a food processor or blender, add the parsley, lemon zest, lemon juice, lima beans, garlic, and 1½ teaspoons kosher salt.
5. Blend until you get a smooth, rich mixture.
6. While blending, drizzle in the olive oil and continue to blend until well-combined.
7. Add the mixture to a large bowl and top with the crumbled bacon.
8. Serve the dip with vegetable sticks and pita chips.

Nutrition:

Calories: 277, fat: 19g, carbs: 18g, protein: 7g, sodium: 422 mg

Artichoke Bean Dip

Preparation time: 5 minutes
Cooking time: 0 minutes
Servings: 4-6

Ingredients

- 1 (7-ounce) artichoke heart, roughly chopped
- 1 teaspoon garlic, minced
- 1 (14-ounce) can cannellini beans, drained; or 5 ounces dry cannellini beans, soaked and cooked
- 2 tablespoons lemon juice
- 1½ tablespoons extra-virgin olive oil
- 1 tablespoon flat-leaf parsley, chopped
- Freshly ground black pepper and kosher salt, to taste
- Extra-virgin olive oil, paprika, and chopped flat-leaf parsley, to garnish
- Pita chips, for serving

Directions

1. In a food processor or blender, add the artichoke hearts, garlic, beans, and lemon juice.
2. Blend until you get a smooth, rich mixture.
3. Add the olive oil while the blender is running, then blend until smooth. Add some water (1-2 tablespoons) if the mixture is too thick.
4. Add the parsley, freshly ground black pepper, and kosher salt. Blend well.
5. Add the mixture to a large bowl and drizzle some more olive oil on top.
6. Cover and refrigerate to chill.
7. When ready to serve, top with the paprika and flat-leaf parsley.
8. Serve with some pita chips.

Nutrition:
Calories: 148, fat: 4g, carbs: 19g, protein: 7g, sodium: 358mg

Garlic Cannellini Bean Spread

Preparation time: 15 minutes
Cooking time: 45 minutes
Servings: 4

Ingredients
- 1 bulb of garlic
- 1¼ teaspoon extra-virgin olive oil
- ¼ cup cilantro leaves, loosely packed
- 1 (15-ounce) can of cannellini/Great Northern beans, drained and rinsed; or 5 ounces dry cannellini/Great Northern beans, soaked and cooked
- ¼ teaspoon kosher salt
- ¼ teaspoon freshly ground black pepper

Directions
1. Preheat the oven to 400F (200C).
2. Peel the bulb of garlic. Using a knife, cut off the top.
3. Place the garlic in a roasting pan and drizzle with 1 teaspoon extra-virgin olive oil to lightly coat.
4. Roast for about 45 minutes. Set aside to cool.
5. In a food processor or blender, add the cooled garlic, cilantro leaves, beans, freshly ground black pepper, and kosher salt.
6. Blend until you get a smooth, rich mixture.
7. Drizzle more olive oil and continue to blend until you get your desired consistency.
8. Serve fresh or cover, refrigerate, and serve chilled.

Nutrition:
Calories: 32, fat: 1g, carbs: 5g, protein: 1g, sodium: 73mg

Cheesy Black Bean Spread

Preparation time: 5 minutes
Cooking time: 0 minutes
Servings: 12

Ingredients
- ½ cup low-fat cottage cheese
- 2 green onions, chopped
- 1 ½ cups dry black beans, soaked and cooked
- 3 tablespoons hot salsa
- 2 cloves garlic, minced
- 1 teaspoon hot pepper sauce
- 1 teaspoon ground coriander
- 2 teaspoons ground cumin
- Freshly ground black pepper and kosher salt, to taste

Directions
1. In a food processor or blender, add the cottage cheese, green onions, black beans, salsa, garlic, hot pepper sauce, ground coriander, ground cumin, freshly ground black pepper, and kosher salt.
2. Blend until you get a smooth, rich mixture.
3. Drizzle some olive oil or water over the mixture and continue to blend until you get your desired consistency.
4. Serve fresh or cover, refrigerate, and serve chilled.

Nutrition:
Calories: 96, fat: 1g, carbs: 16.5g, protein: 7g, sodium: 67mg

Black Bean Corn Fritters

Preparation time: 10 minutes
Cooking time: 10-15 minutes
Servings: 16

Ingredients
- 1 (14-ounce) can black beans, drained and rinsed
- 1 small bunch cilantro, finely chopped
- 1½ cups corn, fresh or frozen (if frozen, make sure to thaw)
- ½ teaspoon ground turmeric, optional
- ½ teaspoon baking powder
- ¾ teaspoon kosher salt
- Freshly ground black pepper, to taste
- 1 cup all-purpose flour or chickpea flour

- ½ cup water
- Extra-virgin olive oil, for frying
- Guacamole, avocado, or dip of your choice

Directions
1. Mash the beans in a medium mixing bowl using a potato masher.
2. Add the corn, cilantro, ground turmeric (if using), baking powder, freshly ground black pepper, kosher salt, and flour.
3. Combine well. Add some water and combine until smooth.
4. In a large pot/deep-frying pan, add oil so it's 1 inch high and heat until shimmering over medium-high heat.
5. Once hot, drop spoonfuls of the mixture into the pan and fry until golden brown, about 2-3 minutes per side.
6. Drain the fat on a plate lined with a paper towel.
7. Serve with guacamole, avocado, or a dip of your choice.

Nutrition:
Calories: 65, fat: 2g, carbs: 9.5g, protein: 2.5g, sodium 212mg

Bean Fritters with Pesto Mayo Dip

Preparation time: 15 minutes
Cooking time: 10 minutes
Servings: 6

Ingredients
- 1 (14-ounce) can cannellini beans, drained and rinsed; or 5 ounces dry cannellini beans, soaked and cooked
- ½ medium zucchini, coarsely grated
- ½ cup corn kernels
- 2 spring onions, finely sliced
- Large handful flat-leaf parsley, roughly chopped
- 1 medium egg
- ⅓ cup plain flour
- Vegetable oil, for frying
- Seasonings of your choice

For the dip:
- 3 tablespoons mayonnaise
- 2 tablespoons crème fraiche
- 2 teaspoons pesto
- Zest from ½ lemon
- Seasonings of your choice

Directions

1. Mash the beans in a large mixing bowl using a potato masher or a fork.
2. Add the zucchini, corn, spring onions, flat-leaf parsley, egg, and flour. Stir to combine, then add the seasonings of your choice. Mix again.
3. Using your hands, form 6 patties from the mixture.
4. In a large pot or deep-frying pan, add oil so it's 1 inch high. Heat the oil on medium-high heat.
5. Once hot, add the patties and fry until golden brown, about 2-3 minutes per side.
6. Drain over plates lined with a paper towel.
7. In a medium mixing bowl, add all the dip ingredients and seasonings of your choice. Combine well.
8. Serve the bean fritters with the prepared dip.

Nutrition:

Calories: 237, fat: 16g, carbs: 15g, protein: 6g, sodium: 428 mg

Chapter 7: Beverages

Blueberry Bean Smoothie

Preparation time: 5 minutes
Cooking time: 0 minutes
Servings: 3-4

Ingredients
- 1 (15.5-ounce) can cannellini beans, drained and rinsed; or 5 ounces dry cannellini beans, soaked and cooked
- 1 medium frozen banana, peeled
- 1 cup frozen blueberries
- ½ cup plain Greek yogurt
- 1½ cups vanilla-flavored almond milk

Directions
1. In a food processor or blender, add all the smoothie ingredients.
2. Blend until you get a smooth, rich mixture.
3. In a tall glass, pour the freshly made smoothie and enjoy.

Nutrition (per cup)
Calories: 360, fat: 1.2g, carbs: 33.5g, protein: 10g, sodium: 352mg

Black Bean Chocolate Smoothie

Preparation time: 5 minutes
Cooking time: 0 minutes
Servings: 2

Ingredients
- 2 bananas, frozen and chopped
- ½ cup cooked black beans (pre-soaked), drained
- 4 Medjool dates, pitted
- 1 tablespoon cashew butter
- 2 tablespoons cocoa/cacao powder
- 1½ cups soy milk or milk of your choice

Directions
1. In a food processor or blender, add all the smoothie ingredients.
2. Blend until you get a smooth, rich mixture.
3. In a tall glass, pour the freshly made smoothie and enjoy.

Nutrition:
Calories: 362, fat: 9g, carbs: 59g, protein: 16g, sodium: 115mg

Chapter 8: Miscellaneous

White Beans
Preparation time: 10 minutes
Cooking time: 35 minutes
Servings: 28

Ingredients:
- 3¼ pounds dried white beans, soaked for 18 hours and drained
- 4½ tsps. salt

Directions:
1. In a Dutch oven, add the beans and enough water to cover them. Turn the heat to high and cook until boiling. Adjust the heat to low then cook for about 30 minutes.
2. Drain the beans and reserve the cooking liquid. In 7 (1-pint) hot sterilized jars, divide the beans and sprinkle with salt.
3. Fill each jar with hot cooking liquid, leaving 1-inch space from the top. Run your knife around the insides of each jar to remove any air bubbles.
4. Wipe any trace of food off the rims of the jars with a clean, moist kitchen towel. Close each jar with a lid and screw on the ring.
5. Carefully place the jars in the pressure canner and process at 10 pounds pressure for about 75 minutes.
6. Remove the jars from the pressure canner and place onto a wooden surface several inches apart to cool completely.
7. After cooling, with your finger, press the top of each jar's lid to ensure that the seal is tight. Store the jars in a cool, dark place.

Nutrition: Calories: 140, fat: 0.5g carbs: 3.2g protein: 11.6g

Pinto Beans Chili
Preparation time: 15 minutes
Cooking time: 40 minutes
Servings: 6

Ingredients
- 2 pounds dry pinto beans, rinsed and drained
- 3–4 bay leaves
- Salt, as needed
- 1 tbsp olive oil
- 2 onions, chopped
- 2 (28-ounce) cans petite diced tomatoes
- 1 (15-ounce) can tomato sauce
- 2 cups beef broth

- 3 tbsps. chili powder
- 2 tbsps. ground cumin
- 2 tsps. garlic powder
- 1 tsps. dried oregano
- 1 tsps. dried thyme
- Ground black pepper, as needed

Directions:
1. In a large stockpot of water, add beans, bay leaves and 1 tablespoon of salt. Place over high heat and cook until boiling. Adjust the heat to low and cook for about 30–35 minutes more.
2. Meanwhile, heat oil in a frying pan over medium heat and sauté the onion for about 4–5 minutes. Drain the beans and return to the same pot.
3. In the pot of beans, add the cooked onion and remaining ingredients and stir to combine. Place the pan over high heat and bring to a boil.
4. In 9 (1-pint) hot sterilized jars, divide the chili, leaving 1-inch space from the top. Run your knife around the insides of each jar to remove any air bubbles.
5. Wipe any trace of food off the rims of jars with a clean, moist kitchen towel. Close each jar with a lid and screw on the ring.
6. Carefully place the jars in the pressure canner and process at 10 pounds pressure for about 90 minutes.
7. Remove the jars from the pressure canner and place onto a wood surface several inches apart to cool completely.
8. After cooling with your finger, press the top of each jar's lid to ensure that the seal is tight. Store the jars in a cool, dark place.

Nutrition: Calories: 220, fat: 2.1g, carbs: 38.5g, protein: 12.9g

Kidney Beans Chili

Preparation time: 15 minutes
Cooking time: 40 minutes
Servings: 7
Ingredients:
- 3 cups dried red kidney beans, soaked overnight and drained
- 1 tbsp salt
- 2 cups onion, chopped
- 1 cup sweet bell pepper, seeded & chopped
- 6 garlic cloves, minced
- ¼ cup fresh parsley, minced
- 8 cups tomato juice
- ½ cup tomato paste
- 3 tbsps. red chili powder
- 1 tsp ground black pepper
- 2 tsps. dried thyme
- 2 tsps. ground cumin

Directions:

1. In a Dutch oven, add the beans and enough water to cover them. Place over high heat and cook until boiling. Adjust the heat to low and cook for about 30 minutes. Drain the beans well.
2. To make the sauce, add the remaining ingredients to a saucepan and place it over medium heat and cook until boiling. Stir in the cooked beans and cook until boiling.
3. In 9 (1-pint) hot sterilized jars, divide the bean mixture. Fill each jar, leaving a 1-inch space from the top.
4. Run your knife around the insides of each jar to remove any air bubbles. Wipe any trace of food off the rims of jars with a clean, moist kitchen towel.
5. Close each jar with a lid and screw on the ring. Carefully place the jars in the pressure canner and process at 10 pounds pressure for about 75 minutes.
6. Remove the jars from the pressure canner and place onto a wood surface several inches apart to cool completely.
7. After cooling with your finger, press the top of each jar's lid to ensure that the seal is tight. Store the jars in a cool, dark place.

Nutrition: Calories: 138, fat: 0.5g, carbs: 27.1g, protein: 8.3g

White Beans & Corn Chili

Preparation time: 15 minutes
Cooking time: 40 minutes
Servings: 8

Ingredients:

- 1-pound white beans, soaked for 6 hours and drained
- 6 cups chicken broth
- 1-pound frozen corn
- 1 medium onion, chopped
- 7 ounces canned green chilies
- 6 garlic cloves
- 4 tsps. ground cumin
- 1 tsp dried oregano
- 2 tsps. cayenne pepper

Directions:

1. In a Dutch oven, add the beans and enough water to cover them. Place over high heat and cook until boiling. Adjust the heat to low and cook for another 30 minutes. Drain the beans completely and set aside.
2. In 7 (1-pint) hot sterilized jars, divide the beans. Fill each jar with hot broth mixture, leaving a 1-inch space from the top.
3. Run your knife around the insides of each jar to remove any air bubbles. Wipe any trace of food off the rims of the jars with a clean, moist kitchen towel.
4. Close each jar with a lid and screw on the ring. Carefully place the jars in the pressure canner and process at 10 pounds pressure for about 75 minutes.

5. Remove the jars from the pressure canner and place onto a wood surface several inches apart to cool completely.
6. After cooling with your finger, press the top of each jar's lid to ensure that the seal is tight. Store these canning jars in a cool, dark place.

Nutrition: Calories: 166 Fat: 2.1 g Carbs: 28.3 g Protein: 11.4 g

Black-Eyed Peas

Preparation time: 10 minutes
Cooking time: 30 minutes
Servings: 7

Ingredients:
- 1½ pounds dried black-eyed peas, soaked overnight and drained
- 6 tbsp. onions, chopped
- 4 tsps. dried thyme
- 1½ tsp kosher salt
- 30 peppercorns

Directions:
1. In a Dutch oven, add the black-eyed peas and enough water to cover them. Place over high heat and cook until boiling. Adjust the heat to low and cook for another 30 minutes.
2. Drain the black-eyed peas and reserve the cooking liquid. In 3 (1-pint) hot sterilized jars, divide the black-eyed peas, onion, thyme, salt, and peppercorn.
3. Fill each jar with hot cooking liquid, leaving 1-inch space from the top. Run your knife around the insides of each jar to remove any air bubbles.
4. Wipe any trace of food off the rims of jars with a clean, moist kitchen towel. Close each jar with a lid and screw on the ring.
5. Carefully place the jars in the pressure canner and process at 10 pounds pressure for about 75 minutes.
6. Remove the jars from the pressure canner and place onto a wood surface several inches apart to cool completely.
7. After cooling with your finger, press the top of each jar's lid to ensure that the seal is tight. Store the jars in a cool, dark place.

Nutrition: Calories: 196, fat: 0.8g, carbs: 34g, protein: 13.6g

Red Lentils

Preparation time: 10 minutes
Cooking time: 10 minutes
Servings: 8

Ingredients:
- 2 cups red lentils, rinsed
- 4 cups chicken broth

- 2 small brown onions, chopped finely

Directions:
1. In a Dutch oven, add lentils, onion, and broth over high heat and cook until boiling. Now set the heat to low and cook for about 5 minutes.
2. In 4 (1-pint) hot sterilized jars, divide the lentils. Fill each jar with hot cooking liquid, leaving 1-inch space from the top.
3. Run your knife around the insides of each jar to remove any air bubbles. Wipe any trace of food off the rims of jars with a clean, moist kitchen towel.
4. Close each jar with a lid and screw on the ring. Carefully place the jars in the pressure canner and process at 10 pounds pressure for about 75 minutes.
5. Remove the jars from the pressure canner and place onto a wood surface several inches apart to cool completely.
6. After cooling with your finger, press the top of each jar's lid to ensure that the seal is tight. Store the jars in a cool, dark place.

Nutrition: Calories: 196 Fat: 1.2 g Carbs: 30.9 g Protein: 15 g

Sweet & Sour Beans

Preparation time: 15 minutes
Cooking time: 30 minutes
Servings: 8

Ingredients:
- 1 pound navy beans
- ½ cup leeks, chopped
- 2 cups water
- 2 cups ketchup
- 1 cup maple syrup
- ½ cup molasses
- 2 tbsp. brown sugar
- 1½ tsp mustard powder
- Salt and ground black pepper, as needed
- ½ cup white vinegar

Directions:
1. In a Dutch oven, add beans and enough water to cover over high heat and cook until boiling. Remove the pan of beans from heat and set aside, covered for about 30–45 minutes.
2. Drain the beans and then add enough fresh water to cover. Add the leeks and cook for about 15–20 minutes. Remove the pan of beans from heat and drain water.
3. In a nonreactive saucepan, add 2 cups of water and remaining ingredients (except for the vinegar) and bring to a gentle boil, stirring continuously.

4. Remove the pan of cooking mixture from heat and stir in the vinegar. In 4 (1-pint) hot sterilized jars, divide the beans. Fill each jar with hot vinegar mixture, leaving 1-inch space from the top.
5. Run your knife around the insides of each jar to remove any air bubbles. Wipe any trace of food off the rims of jars with a clean, moist kitchen towel.
6. Close each jar with a lid and screw on the ring. Carefully place the jars in the pressure canner and process at 10 pounds pressure for about 75 minutes.
7. Remove the jars from the pressure canner and place onto a wood surface several inches apart to cool completely.
8. After cooling with your finger, press the top of each jar's lid to ensure that the seal is tight. Store the jars in a cool, dark place.

Nutrition: Calories: 389, fat: 1.1g, carbs: 85.1g, protein: 13.7g

Baked Beans

Preparation time: 15 minutes
Cooking time: 12 minutes
Servings: 6

Ingredients:
- 1-pound dried navy beans
- 2 bay leaves
- 1 cup onion, chopped finely
- 6 tbsps. tomato paste
- 3 tbsps. brown sugar
- 1½ tbsp Worcestershire sauce
- 1½ tsp mustard powder
- 1½ tsp salt
- 1½ tsp ground black pepper

Directions:
1. In a Dutch oven, add beans and enough water to cover over high heat and cook until boiling. Remove the pan of beans from heat and set aside, covered for about 1 hour.
2. Drain the beans and then add enough fresh water to cover. In the pan of beans, add bay leaves over high heat and cook until boiling. Boil for about 2 minutes. Drain the beans, reserving the cooking liquid.
3. To make the sauce, in a large microwave-safe bowl, add remaining ingredients and stir to combine. Add reserved 3 cups of hot cooking liquid and microwave for about 5 minutes.
4. Remove the bowl of sauce from the microwave and mix well. In 3 (1-pint) hot sterilized jars, divide the beans. Fill each jar with hot sauce mixture, leaving 1-inch space from the top.
5. Run your knife around the insides of each jar to remove any air bubbles. Wipe any trace of food off the rims of jars with a clean, moist kitchen towel.

6. Close each jar with a lid and screw on the ring. Carefully place the jars in the pressure canner and process at 10 pounds pressure for about 75 minutes.
7. Remove the jars from the pressure canner and place onto a wood surface several inches apart to cool completely.
8. After cooling with your finger, press the top of each jar's lid to ensure that the seal is tight. Store the jars in a cool, dark place.

Nutrition: Calories: 300, fat: 1.1g, carbs: 56.6g, protein: 18.2g

Baked Navy Beans

Preparation time: 15 minutes
Cooking time: 4 hours & 45 minutes
Servings: 6 jars

Ingredients:
- 4 cups dried navy beans or peas
- 8 oz salt pork, cut into bits
- 4 medium-large onions
- 2/3 Cup brown sugar
- 2 tsps dry mustard
- 2 tsps dry salt
- 2/3 Cup molasses

Directions:
1. Wash beans and cover with water. Leave it in a cool place for twelve to eighteen hours. Drain the beans and then pour them into a large saucepan and add twelve cups of water. Place over medium-high heat.
2. Allow it to boil. Reduce heat and simmer covered slowly until bean skins start cracking. Drain beans and keep the liquid.
3. Pour drained beans inside a baking dish. Add onions, pork, and salt. In a separate container, combine mustard, molasses, and brown sugar with four cups of reserved cooking fluid. Add more water if necessary.
4. Add sauce to the beans, cover and bake at 350°F for approx. 3 hours 30 minutes.
5. Ladle hot prepared baked beans into each canning jar. Remember to leave a one-inch headspace. Use a spatula to remove air bubbles, then use a clean cloth to wipe jar rims, after that, adjust lids, and screw band.
6. Set the filled jars in a pressure canner at 11 pounds pressure for dial-gauge or 10 pounds for the weighted-gauge canner.
7. Process the jars for 75 minutes, adjusting for altitude. Switch off the heat and let pressure drop naturally.
8. Remove the lid and cool the jars in the canner for 2 minutes. Take out the jars and cool. Inspect lids seal after twenty-four hours.

Nutrition: Calories: 167, carbs: 25g, fat: 4g, protein: 9g

Shelled Peas

Preparation time: 15 minutes
Cooking time: 40 minutes
Servings: 4

Ingredients:
- Shell peas, as needed

Directions:
1. Place a large saucepan over medium-high heat, add the peas and cover with water. Leave to boil. Boil medium peas for five minutes and small peas for three minutes.
2. Remove from the heat and drain. Rinse in warm water and then re-drain. Pack the hot peas loosely into each canning jar, add seasoning and freshly boiled water
3. Remember to leave one-inch of room at the top. Use a spatula to remove air bubbles, then use a clean cloth to wipe the rims of the jars, after that, screw the lids on tightly.
4. Place the filled jars in a pressure canner at 11 pounds pressure for dial-gauge or 10 pounds for the weighted-gauge canner. Process the jars for 40 minutes, adjusting for altitude. Switch off the heat and let pressure drop naturally. Remove the lid and cool the jars in the canner for 2 minutes. Take the jars out and let them cool. Inspect the seals after twenty-four hours.

Nutrition: Calories: 87, carbs: 10g, fat: 1g, protein: 7g

Dried Beans

Preparation time: 15 minutes
Cooking time: 1 hour and 15 minutes
Servings: 4

Ingredients:
- 1-pound dried beans, such as cannellini, kidney, pinto black, or a mixture
- Approx. 2 liters water
- 1 bay leaf
- Salt (optional)

Directions:
1. Wash and rinse the beans. In a large container, cover the beans with cool water and soak for twelve hours.
2. Wash and drain the beans. Place a large saucepan over medium-high heat. Add the beans and the bay leaf. Add in enough water to cover the beans. Bring to a boil, reduce the heat and let them cook slowly for 30 minutes.
3. Drain the beans with a strainer. Remove the bay leaf and reserve the cooking liquid.

4. Pack the beans into each canning jar and add the reserved cooking liquid. Remember to leave a one-inch space at the top.
5. Use a small spatula to remove any air bubbles, then use a clean cloth to wipe the rims, after that, screw the lids on tightly.
6. Place the filled jars in a pressure canner at 11 pounds pressure for dial-gauge or 10 pounds for the weighted-gauge canner.
7. Process the jars for 75 minutes. Switch off the heat and let the pressure drop naturally.
8. Remove the lid and cool the jars in the canner for 5 minutes. Take the jars out and let them cool. Inspect the seals after twenty-four hours.

Nutrition: Calories: 150, carbs: 12g, fat: 0g, protein: 5g

Beans with Pork

Preparation time: 15 minutes
Cooking time: 1 hour and 30 minutes
Servings: 4

Ingredients:
- 4 lbs. white beans, dried
- 2 quarts tomato juice
- 1 lb. salt pork or bacon
- ¼ lb. brown sugar
- ½ bottle ketchup
- ½ cup molasses
- ½ tsp cinnamon
- ½ tsp ground mustard
- ½ tsp salt
- ¼ tsp red pepper or cayenne pepper

Directions:
1. Soak the beans overnight. Wash and cook the beans for twenty minutes over medium-high heat. Remove the beans from heat, drain and combine them with the rest of the ingredients.
2. Pack the beans into each canning jar. Remember to leave a one-inch space from the top. Use a small spatula to remove any air bubbles and then use a clean cloth to wipe jar rims; tightly screw on the lids.
3. Set the filled jars in a pressure canner at 11 pounds pressure for dial-gauge or 10 pounds for the weighted-gauge canner. Process the jars for 90 minutes.
4. Switch off the heat and let the pressure drop naturally. Remove the lid and cool the jars in the canner for 5 minutes. Take out the jars and cool. Inspect the seals after twenty-four hours.

Nutrition: Calories: 350, carbs: 63g, fat: 4g, protein: 16g

Cranberry Beans

Preparation time: 15 minutes
Cooking time: 60 minutes
Servings: 4

Ingredients:
- 4 lbs. unshelled cranberry beans (2 pounds, shelled)
- 3 garlic cloves, chopped
- ¾ cup white wine
- 4 tbsp lemon juice
- 6 tbsp olive oil
- 6 tsp fresh marjoram or 3 tsp dried one
- ½ tsp black pepper, freshly ground
- ¾ tsp salt
- 2 cups chicken stock

Directions:
1. In a large container, combine the beans with all the other ingredients except for the chicken stock. Pack the beans into each canning jar and add chicken broth.
2. Remember to leave a one-inch space from the top. Use a small spatula to remove air bubbles, then use a clean cloth to wipe the rims of the jars. Next screw the lids on the jars tightly.
3. Place the filled jars in a pressure canner at 11 pounds pressure for dial-gauge or 10 pounds for the weighted-gauge canner. Process the jars for 60 minutes.
4. Switch off the heat and let the pressure drop naturally. Remove the lid and cool the jars in the canner for 5 minutes. Take out the jars and let them cool. Inspect the seals after twenty-four hours.

Nutrition: Calories: 147, carbs: 44g, fat: 0g, protein: 15g

Perfect Morning Bean Eggs

Preparation time: 8-10 minutes
Cooking time: 15 minutes
Servings: 4

Ingredients
- 2 tablespoons unsalted butter
- 2 medium garlic cloves, finely chopped
- 1 medium onion, finely chopped
- 2 tablespoons light brown sugar
- 2 (15.5-ounce) cans cannellini beans, drained and rinsed; or 5 ounces dry cannellini beans, soaked and cooked
- ½ cup ketchup
- 2 teaspoons Worcestershire sauce

- ½ cup water
- Freshly ground black pepper and kosher salt, to taste
- 1 tablespoon olive oil
- 4 large eggs
- 4 slices bread, toasted

Directions

1. In a medium saucepan or skillet, heat the butter over medium heat until melted.
2. Add in the onion and garlic. Cook until softened, about 3-4 minutes.
3. Mix in the brown sugar, beans, ketchup, Worcestershire sauce, and water. Simmer for 5 minutes or until the mixture thickens.
4. Season to taste with freshly ground black pepper and salt, then remove from heat.
5. In another medium saucepan or skillet, heat oil over medium heat.
6. Crack the eggs, adding more pepper and salt to taste. Cook until yolks are runny, and whites are set.
7. Over the toasted bread, add the bean mixture and top with the eggs.
8. Serve warm.

Nutrition:
Calories: 470, fat: 14g, carbs: 56g, protein: 21g, sodium: 701mg

Tahini Bean Hummus

Preparation time: 15 minutes
Cooking time: 0 minutes
Servings: 5

Ingredients
- 1 (15-ounce) can white beans/butter beans, drained and rinsed; or 5 ounces dry white beans/butter beans, soaked and cooked
- 1 garlic clove, minced
- 1 ice cube
- 1 teaspoon ground cumin
- ½ teaspoon ground coriander
- ½ teaspoon crushed red pepper flakes
- Juice of ½ lemon
- ¼ cup tahini
- Kosher salt, to taste
- Extra-virgin olive oil, for drizzling
- Lime juice, optional

Directions
1. In a food processor or blender, add the beans and garlic.
2. Blend until you get a smooth, rich mixture.

3. Add the ice cube, ground cumin, ground coriander, lemon juice, tahini, and salt; blend for 3-4 more minutes until smooth.
4. Season to taste with kosher salt, freshly ground black pepper, and lime juice. Serve fresh or refrigerate and serve chilled.
5. Serve with a drizzle of olive oil on top.

Nutrition:
Calories: 2221, fat: 12.5g, carbs: 21g, protein: 8.5g, sodium: 248 mg

Sweet Potato Bean Breakfast Bowl

Preparation time: 5 minutes
Cooking time: 15 minutes
Servings: 4

Ingredients
- 4 tablespoons olive oil
- ½ yellow onion, diced
- 1 red bell pepper, cored and sliced
- 3 cups sweet potato, diced
- Freshly ground black pepper and kosher salt, to taste
- ½ tablespoon paprika
- 1 teaspoon ground cumin
- 2 cups spinach, torn into small pieces
- 1 (15-ounce) can black beans, drained and rinsed; or 5 ounces dry black beans, soaked and cooked

Directions
1. In a medium saucepan, heat the oil over medium heat.
2. Add in the bell pepper, onion, and sweet potato, then season with freshly ground black pepper and salt.
3. Add the ground cumin and paprika. Cook until softened, about 8-10 minutes.
4. Add the spinach and cook until wilted, about 4-5 minutes.
5. Add the beans and combine well.
6. Serve the beans with the toppings of your choice (sliced avocado, cooked eggs, toast, etc.)

Nutrition:
Calories: 353, fat: 14g, carbs: 50g, protein: 9g, sodium: 287 mg

Black Bean Omelet

Preparation time: 5 minutes
Cooking time: 10-15 minutes
Servings: 4

Ingredients

- Juice of 1 lime
- ¼ teaspoon ground cumin
- 1 can (14 to 16 ounces) black beans, drained and rinsed
- Hot sauce, to taste
- 1 tablespoon olive oil or butter
- 8 large eggs
- Freshly ground black pepper and salt, to taste
- ½ cup feta cheese, plus more for serving
- "Pico de gallo" or bottled/canned salsa
- 1 avocado, pitted and sliced, optional

Directions

1. In a blender or food processor, blend the lime juice, ground cumin, beans, and hot sauce. Blend until you get the consistency of refried beans. Add some water if the mixture is too thick.
2. In a medium saucepan or skillet, heat oil or butter over medium heat.
3. Crack two eggs into the pan. Using a spatula, stir gently keeping the egg in a circle shape. Cook on one side, flip, then cook on the other side. Cook until the eggs are well-set.
4. Add ¼ of the bean mixture and 2 tablespoons of the feta cheese to the center, then fold the omelet to cover the bean mixture.
5. Set aside on a serving plate.
6. Repeat the same process to make another omelet using the remaining ingredients.
7. Serve warm.

Nutrition:
Calories: 330, fat: 8g, carbs: 46g, protein: 23.5g, sodium: 480mg

Avocado Black Bean Eggs

Preparation time: 5 minutes
Cooking time: 5 minutes
Servings: 2

Ingredients
2 teaspoons grapeseed oil
1 large garlic clove, sliced
1 red chili pepper, seeded and thinly sliced
2 large eggs
1 (14-ounce) can black beans (do not drain); or 5 ounces dry black beans, soaked and cooked
1 (14-ounce) can cherry tomatoes
¼ teaspoon cumin seeds

1 small avocado, pitted, halved, and sliced
A handful of cilantros, chopped
1 lime, cut into wedges

Directions
1. In a large saucepan or skillet, heat the oil over medium heat.
2. Add in the garlic and chili pepper. Cook until fragrant and softened.
3. On one side of the pan, crack the eggs and cook until they begin to set.
4. Add the beans with their juices and stir gently.
5. Add the tomatoes and cumin seeds. Cook until beans are warmed through, then remove from the heat.
6. On serving plates, arrange the avocado slices and cilantro. Top with the bean mixture.
7. Squeeze the lime wedges on top and serve warm with additional lime wedges, optional.

Nutrition:
Calories: 356, fat: 20g, carbs: 18g, protein: 20g, sodium: 804 mg

Baked Feta Bean Tomatoes

Preparation time:10 minutes.
Cooking time: 40 minutes.
Servings: 4

Ingredients
- 2 tablespoons tomato paste
- 1 (14-ounce) can butter beans, drained, and rinsed; or 5 ounces dry butter beans, soaked and cooked
- 1 (14-ounce) can chickpeas, drained and rinsed; or 5 ounces dry chickpeas, soaked and cooked
- 6 garlic cloves, peeled
- 14 ounces heirloom tomatoes, chopped so they're all roughly the same size
- 4 ½ ounces cherry truss tomatoes
- 2 teaspoons smoked paprika
- ¼ cup extra-virgin olive oil
- 2 tablespoons pomegranate molasses
- 3 ½ ounces Greek feta cheese, crumbled
- Tabasco and sliced baguettes, to serve

Directions
1. Preheat the oven to 425F (220C).
2. Grease a baking dish with cooking spray or cooking oil.
3. To the baking dish, add the tomato paste, butter beans, chickpeas, garlic, tomatoes, paprika, 2 tablespoons oil, and 1½ tablespoons molasses.

4. Bake until tomatoes soften, about 30 minutes.
5. Stir to break tomatoes gently, then bake for 10 more minutes until tomatoes start to release juices.
6. Remove from the oven and drizzle the remaining oil and molasses over the tomatoes. Top with the feta cheese.
7. Serve with Tabasco and sliced baguettes.

Nutrition: Calories: 314, fat: 18g, carbs: 23g, protein: 14g, sodium: 854mg

White Bean Avocado Toast

Preparation time: 5 minutes
Cooking time: 20 minutes
Servings: 4

Ingredients
- 1 tablespoon olive oil
- 3 cloves garlic, minced
- 1 (15-ounce) can cannellini beans (white kidney beans), drained and rinsed; or 5 ounces dry cannellini beans, soaked and cooked
- ½ teaspoon kosher salt, or to taste
- Freshly ground black pepper, to taste
- ½ teaspoon dried oregano
- 2 avocados, pitted, peeled, and chopped
- 4 slices hearty whole-grain bread, toasted
- BBQ sauce, to taste
- Hemp seeds, to taste

Directions
1. In a medium saucepan or skillet, heat the oil over medium heat.
2. Add the garlic and cook until fragrant, about 1-2 minutes.
3. Add the beans, freshly ground black pepper, salt, and oregano. Cook for 4-5 minutes.
4. In a small bowl, mash the chopped avocado.
5. Spread the mashed avocado evenly over the bread slices, then top with the bean mixture.
6. Top with the BBQ sauce and hemp seeds, then serve.

Nutrition:
Calories: 327, fat: 7g, carbs: 52g, protein: 15g, sodium: 142mg

Kale Bean Potato Hash

Preparation time: 5 minutes
Cooking time: 15 minutes
Servings: 4-5

Ingredients
- 3 medium Yukon Gold potatoes, diced into ½ inch cubes
- 1 tablespoon avocado oil
- ½ red bell pepper, cored and diced
- ½ cup vegan breakfast sausage, chopped, optional
- 2 cloves garlic, minced
- ½ large onion, finely diced
- ½ (8-ounce) can black beans, drained and rinsed; or 2.5 ounces dry black beans, soaked and cooked
- 2 heaping cups kale, stemmed and chopped
- 1 teaspoon Old Bay seasoning, or to taste
- Freshly ground black pepper and kosher salt, to taste
- A handful of cilantro or flat-leaf parsley, finely chopped
- 1 large avocado, pitted and sliced, to serve
- Toasted bread, to serve

Directions
1. Cook the potatoes in boiling water for 4-5 minutes; drain and set aside.
2. In a medium saucepan or skillet, heat oil over medium heat.
3. Add the potatoes and cook until browned, about 4-5 minutes.
4. Add the bell pepper, vegan sausage, garlic, onion, and Old Bay seasoning. Mix until well-combined.
5. Cook for 8-10 minutes until potatoes are cooked through.
6. Add the beans and kale; cook until kale wilts, about 2 minutes.
7. Season with freshly ground black pepper and salt, then top with the chopped cilantro/parsley.
8. Serve warm with the toasted bread and avocado slices.

Nutrition:
Calories 149, fat 3 g, carbs 26.5 g, Protein 5 g, sodium 228 mg

Conclusion

There are so many ways to cook beans using different appliances. I mainly cook my beans in a slow cooker. The slow simmering produces a rich broth that my family loves. I also love to cook beans on the stove for a great depth of flavor. Garbanzo beans cooked on the stove produce a rich broth and I use the broth in place of chicken broth in some recipes. I always use the high setting when cooking beans in the slow cooker. Cooking on low takes much longer.

There are also numerous appliances available to cook rice. I personally use the stove top or a slow cooker to cook rice. I like to use the slow cooker since I can prepare large quantities of rice for the freezer.

I use canned beans or home cooked beans for most of my recipes. Listed below is some important quantity conversation information for beans.

1 lb. of dried beans equals 2 cups of dry beans or about 6 cups of cooked beans.

A can of drained beans equals about 1 1/2 cups of dry beans.

Cooked beans can be frozen for up to 3 months. I freeze my beans in 2 cup increments. You can freeze the beans with or without the cooking liquid. To thaw frozen beans, place them in the microwave on the defrost setting or place the beans in the refrigerator overnight. Dried beans can be stored for up to 6 months. Some say you can keep them longer but I find the beans do not soften upon cooking. Canned beans may be kept for up to 1 year in a cool pantry.

Some say do not add salt or seasonings to your beans until the beans are fully cooked. I add my seasonings to the beans when I start cooking them. The seasonings add a depth of flavor to both the beans and the broth.

Most beans can be substituted for another bean in any given recipe. Pinto beans, great northern beans, navy beans and black beans are good substitutes for each other. The flavors will be slightly different especially with black beans. My family does not seem to mind the changes. I add 2 cups of pinto beans, lentils, red kidney beans, black beans or great northern beans to spaghetti sauce for extra nutrition and fiber. Adding beans to spaghetti and reducing the meat was a key in getting my family to eat less meat.

Seasoning really complements beans so be generous with your seasoning. Salt, black pepper, cumin, onion, powder, garlic powder, oregano, chili powder and basil work well with beans. Do not add tomatoes or acidic foods until the beans are almost fully cooked. The acidic nature will toughen the skin on the beans. Follow the recipe guidelines for best results.

Add cooked beans to salads for extra protein. I reduce the meat in dishes and add 1 cup cooked beans. Reducing the meat by 1/4 in a recipe and adding 1/2 cup cooked beans is a great way to introduce beans to your family. Slowly increase the beans and reduce the meat and your family will soon not notice the difference.

There are several methods for soaking beans. I always soak beans before cooking. It does help eliminate gas and the cooking time is also reduced. Do not soak dried black eye peas, lentils or green peas.

Traditional Soak

Add the beans to a pot with a lid. For every cup of dry beans, add 2 cups of cold water. Place a lid on the pot and soak the beans for at least 12 hours but no longer than 24 hours. I regularly soak pinto and great northern beans for 24 hours. You will see bubbles form on top of the water and this means the gas is being released from the beans. Do not soak beans for longer than 24 hours or they may start sprouting.

Quick Soak

For every cup of dried beans, add 2 cups of cold water to a large pot. Place the pot on the stove over medium high heat. Bring the beans to a boil and boil for 2 minutes. Remove the beans from the heat and place a lid on the pot. Let the beans soak for 1 hour.

Refrigerator Soak

Dried beans can be soaked for up to 48 hours in the refrigerator. For every cup of dried beans, add 3 cups of cold water to the pot. Keep the beans covered while soaking.

Rice Cooking Tips

Always bring the water to a boil before adding the rice. It is important to cook rice with a lid on the sauce pan. The rice will absorb the water and cook evenly. You can cook rice without a lid on the pan, but you will need to add more water to the recipe and the cooking time may be longer. The rice may also be mushier if cooked this way. Only cook until the rice is tender or the rice will be gummy.

When cooking rice for a savory dish or rice bowls, I always cook the rice in vegetable or chicken broth and add onion and garlic to the rice while cooking for extra flavor. You can also try cooking the rice in wine, beer or fruit juices to achieve different flavors. Keep dried minced onion and jarred minced garlic on hand to add to rice.

Add a few drops of Tabasco sauce to the boiling water when cooking rice to perk up the flavor of the rice. Adding 2 teaspoons of vinegar to the boiling can also give the rice a better flavor. You can also use fresh lemon juice instead of vinegar.

Do not stir the rice after it comes to a boil. It will make the rice gummy.

Cooked rice will keep about 5 days in the refrigerator. You can freeze cooked rice for 3 months. Freezing rice makes it handy to use in recipes. I freeze rice in 1 cup portion sizes. You do not have to thaw the rice if you are using it in a casserole or main dish. To reheat rice, add 2 tablespoons of water to each cup of leftover rice. Heat the rice in a microwave or in a saucepan. Place the pan over low heat and let the rice simmer until hot and fluffy.

Do not leave cooked rice in the pan for more than 10 minutes. The rice will start to cool and gel. This makes for really unappetizing rice. Remember you can use leftover rice to thicken soups instead of flour or cornstarch. Some find that rice is bland and needs a lot of seasonings, so be generous when seasoning with herbs and spices.

Made in the USA
Las Vegas, NV
03 October 2024

96224497R00072